# FRANKENSTEIN'S CASTLE

By the same author:

THE OUTSIDER
RELIGION AND THE REBEL
THE AGE OF DEFEAT
THE STRENGTH TO DREAM
BEYOND THE OUTSIDER
THE PHILOSOPHER'S STONE
THE OCCULT
MYSTERIES

# COLIN WILSON

# *Frankenstein's Castle*

### THE DOUBLE BRAIN:
### DOOR TO WISDOM

ASHGROVE PRESS, SEVENOAKS

Published in Great Britain by
ASHGROVE PRESS
25 Quakers Hall Lane
Sevenoaks, Kent TN13 3TU

ISBN 0 906798 11 6

First published 1980

Photoset in 11/13 Plantin by
Galleon Photosetting, Ipswich
Printed and bound by
Billing and Sons Limited
Guildford, London, Oxford, Worcester

*For Tony Britton*
*with affection*

# Acknowledgements

I wish to acknowledge the help of Eddie Campbell, who not only suggested the writing of this book but offered many hints and suggestions. Also of two American correspondents, Dennis Stacy and Stephen Spickard, who went to a great deal of trouble to obtain for me details of the Basa case. Finally, my thanks to Idries Shah, for drawing my attention to Ornstein's work on the split brain.

CW

# Contents

The case of Teresita Basa, and the 'possession' of Mrs Chua. Is personality a part of the structure of the brain? The case of Jasbir Lal Jat. The case of Lurancy Verrum. The case of Louis Vivé. Christine Beauchamp and 'Sally'. Doris Fischer and 'Margaret'. Levels of personality? Different brain patterns of the 'personalities'. Galton induces 'persecution mania'. James and automatic writing. Is the left a villain? Hesse's 'Russian Man'. *The Dam Busters* and the 'two beams' of consciousness. Gibbon and the *Decline and Fall*. 'Forgetfulness' of existence. What has gone wrong with human evolution? We fail to make proper use of consciousness. The alliance of the left-brain and the robot: how it operates. Dürrenmatt's Angel and Green's whiskey priest. How can we break through to a new evolutionary level?

Ward's *Drug Taker's Notes*: 'a state of consciousness already more complete than the fullest degree of ordinary awareness'. Disappearance of the sense of time. The role of serotinin. The pineal gland. The brain is a Frankenstein's Castle. The right-brain as criminal. Huxley and mescalin. The drawbacks. The 'bad trip'. My own mescalin experience. The objection to psychedelics. Cossery's advocacy of hashish in *A Room in Cairo*. The objections. Julian Jaynes and his theory of the 'bicameral mind'. The development of the left-brain ego. Jean-Jacques Rousseau and the rejection of 'civilisation'. Freud's *Civilisation and Its Discontents*. De Sade unintentionally demonstrates the fallacy in the 'rejection' argument. How to avoid being trapped in left-brain consciousness. Hans Selye and stress. Coué, Schult and Liébault. Auto-suggestion and its power to repair the homeostatic system. Kamiya and bio-feedback. Neil Miller's trained rats. The objections to bio-feedback as a solution: James and the Chautauqua Community. Aleister Crowley and Jane Wolfe. Crowley's limitations. Jacob Boehme's mystical vision. Robert Graves and 'The Abominable Mr Gunn'. Plotinus. The dual ego.

cancer patients. Is thought independent of the brain? The 'Unit of Pure Thought'. The inner phantasmagoria. The computer. Is Miller merely echoing Husserl? My own insight into the 'controlling ego'. The two Irish navvies. Hemingway's 'Soldier's Home'. The ladder of selves. Habit-neurosis. D. H. Lawrence and his objections to the personal ego. Forgetfulness – Nietzsche's cows. Yeats and Michelangelo. Frankl's prisoners at Dachau. The power of suggestion. Maslow and his students. The hosepipe and the garden tap. The flatworm experiment again. The mechanism of 'life failure'. Failure of the 'triple-alliance'. The ego is to blame. The fatal alliance of instinct and robot. Why does the split-brain operation make so little difference? Mozart and creativity. The vicious circle. Graham Greene and the 'Revolver in the Corner Cupboard'. The housewife who discovered she was free. Human beings are like grandfather clocks driven by watchsprings. The 'if-only' feeling. 'To be free is nothing; to become free is heaven'. The broken spring. Ramakrishna and samadhi. Summary: the newness of the triple alliance. Ramakrishna's grass-eating tiger. Alienation and self-division: Kierkegaard, Camus and Sartre. My own analysis.

# FRANKENSTEIN'S CASTLE

# ONE

# The 'Other Mode'

AS I APPROACH the age of fifty – just twice the age at which my first book, *The Outsider*, appeared – I realise more clearly than ever that my life has been dominated by a single obsession: a search for what I call 'the other mode of consciousness'.

An example will clarify my meaning.

A musician friend once told me how he had returned home after a hard day's work feeling rather tired and depressed. He poured himself a whisky, and put a record on the gramophone – it was a suite of dances by Praetorius. As he drank the whisky, he began to relax. Suddenly, he says, he 'took off'. The music and the whisky entered into some kind of combination that produced a feeling of wild happiness, a rising tide of sheer exhilaration.

Why describe this as 'another mode' of consciousness, rather than simply as ordinary consciousness transformed by happiness? Because it can lead to experiences that seem completely beyond the range of 'normal' consciousness. A BBC producer friend told me how he had sat in an empty control room at the BBC and played himself a record of the Schubert Octet, which happened to be on the turntable. Suddenly, he said, he *became* Schubert. I was intrigued and tried to get him to be more precise. Did he have a kind of 'time slip' into Schubert's Vienna, so he knew what Schubert had eaten for lunch on the day he started composing? No, this was not what he meant. He tried to explain: that he had felt as if he was *composing* the music, so that he could understand why Schubert had written each bar as he had, and precisely what he might put into the next bar. . . . I saw that what he was describing was not a mystical or 'occult' experience, but simply an unusually deep sense of empathy. Sartre once said that to enjoy a book is to rewrite it; my friend had done the same for Schubert's Octet. We are bound to 'enter into' music if it is to be more than just a meaningless noise; but clearly, my friend had entered into it ten times as deeply as usual, like going down in a lift.

But then, perhaps it is a mistake to emphasise this element of empathy or sympathy. I had a similar experience when writing a book about Bernard Shaw. A friend had borrowed a book that I wanted to consult; and on this particular morning, he returned it. So I sat down at my typewriter feeling pleased I had it back. It was a pleasant, warm day, with the sun streaming through on to my desk. I was writing the chapter about Shaw's marriage and 'breakthrough', after years of plodding around London's theatres and concert halls as a critic. No doubt I was 'identifying' with Shaw, imagining what it must have been like to feel that you have sailed out of a storm into a quiet harbour. But this was not what explained that sudden feeling of intense joy, as if my heart had turned into a balloon and was sailing up into the air. It was not just Shaw's life that was somehow passing through my mind; it was something bigger: a sense of the multiplicity of life itself. In a sense, I was back in Edwardian London; but it could just as easily have been Goethe's Weimar or Mozart's Salzburg.

In fact, this 'other mode' of consciousness is a state of *perception* rather than empathy – an awareness of a wider range of 'fact' – of the actuality of the world outside me. What has changed in such experiences is our perspective. I am used to seeing the world in what might be called 'visual perspective' – that is, with the objects closest to me looking realler and larger than the objects in the middle distance, which in turn look realler and larger than the objects on the horizon. In these experiences, we seem to sail up above this visual perspective, and the objects on the horizon are as real as my fingers and toes.

This is the experience that lay at the heart of *The Outsider*. The 'Romantic Outsiders' – Rousseau, Shelley, Hoffmann, Hölderlin, Berlioz, Wagner, Dostoevsky, Van Gogh, Nietzsche – were always experiencing flashes of the 'other mode' of consciousness, with its tantalising hint of a new *kind* of perception, in which distant realities are as real as the present moment. But this created a new problem: intense dissatisfaction with the ordinary form of consciousness, with its emphasis on the immediate and the trivial. So the rate of death by suicide or tuberculosis was alarmingly high among writers and artists of the nineteenth century. Many of them seemed to feel that this was inevitable: that death and despair were the price you paid for these flashes of the 'other mode'. Even a relatively latecomer to the scene like Thomas Mann continued to think of the problem in terms of these bleak opposites: stupidity *and* health, or intensity *and* death.

I was inclined to question this equation. In many cases, the misery seemed self-inflicted. Eliot was right when he snapped: 'Shelley was a fool.' Shelley was a fool to fall in love with every pretty face that came by, a fool to believe England could be improved by violent revolution, a fool to give way to self-pity every time he got depressed, and to feel that the situation could be improved by 'lying down like a weary child to weep away this life of care'. The same criticism applies to a large number of 'romantic outsiders'.

Still, even when full allowance was made for weakness and self-pity, there was another problem that could not be dismissed so easily. L. H. Myers had called it 'the near and the far' (in the novel of that title). The young Prince Jali gazes out over the desert in the light of the setting sun, and reflects that there are two deserts, 'one that was a glory for the eye, another that it was a weariness to trudge' – the near and the far. And the horizon, with all its promise, is always 'the far'. The near is trivial and boring. Huysmans had made the same point amusingly in *A Rebours*, where, after reading Dickens, the hero, Des Esseintes, has a sudden craving for London. While waiting for his train he goes to the English tavern near the Gare St Lazare, and eats roast beef and potatoes, and drinks pints of ale. Then it strikes him that he has, so to speak, tasted the essence of England, and that 'it would be madness to risk spoiling such unforgettable experiences with a clumsy change of locality'. So he takes a cab back home.

Yet Myers had also glimpsed an answer when he made Jali reflect: 'Yes, one day he would be vigorous enough in breath and stride to capture the promise of the horizon.' He may not have believed it himself, but it was still the correct answer: vitality. In 1960, my conviction was confirmed by the work of an American professor of psychology, Abraham Maslow. Maslow said he had got tired of studying sick people because they never talked about anything but their illness; so he decided to study healthy people instead. He soon made an interesting discovery: that healthy people frequently had 'peak experiences' – flashes of immense happiness. For example, a young mother was watching her husband and children eating breakfast when a beam of sunlight came through the window. It suddenly struck her how lucky she was, and she went into the peak experience – the 'other mode'. Maslow made another interesting discovery. When he talked to his students about peak experiences, they began recollecting peak experiences which they had had, but which they had often overlooked at the time. Moreover, as soon as they began thinking about and discussing peak experiences, *they began having them regularly*. In other words: the peak experience, the moment when the near and the far seem to come together, *is* a product of vitality and optimism. But it can also be amplified or repeated through *reflection*, by turning the full attention upon it instead of allowing it merely to 'happen'.

The case of the young mother reinforces the point. She was happy as she watched her husband and children eating, but it was an unreflective happiness. The beam of sunlight made her feel: 'I am happy', and instantly intensified it. It is as though we possessed a kind of mirror inside us, a mirror which has the power to turn 'things that happen' into *experience*. It seems that thought itself has a power for which it has never been given credit.

This was a major discovery. It meant that – contrary to the belief of the romantics – the 'other mode' *is* within our control. Shelley asked the 'spirit of beauty':

'Why dost thou pass away and leave our state,
This dim vast vale of tears, vacant and desolate?'

The answer, in Shelley's case, was clearly that he went around with the assumption that human existence *is* a 'dim vast vale of tears', and regarded the peak experiences as visitations of 'the awful shadow of some unseen power' – instead of recognising that the unseen power lay within himself.

What we are speaking about is what Gottfried Benn called 'primal perception', that sudden sense of 'matchless clarity' that gives the world a 'new-minted' look. We find it in the sharp outlines of Japanese art, with its white mountain peaks and electric blue skies. T. E. Lawrence describes one in *Seven Pillars of Wisdom:*

'We started out on one of those clear dawns that wake up the senses with the sun, while the intellect, tired after the thinking of the night, was yet abed. For an hour or two, on such a morning, the sounds, scents and colours of the world struck man individually and directly, not filtered through or made typical by thought: they seemed to exist sufficiently by themselves . . .'

Lawrence has also put his finger on the reason that we experience 'primal perception' so infrequently: the *filter* of thought, of the mind's expectations. It could also be described as the robot, the mechanical part of us. Our 'robot' is invaluable; it takes over difficult tasks – like driving the car or talking a foreign language – and does them far more easily and efficiently than when we are doing them consciously. But it also 'gets used' to spring mornings and Mozart symphonies, destroying 'the glory and the freshness' that makes the child's world so interesting. The robot may be essential to human life; but he makes it hardly worth living.

The robot seems to be located in the brain. This is clear

from the effects of psychedelic drugs like LSD and mescalin, which apparently achieve their effect by paralysing certain 'chemical messengers' in the brain. The result is certainly a form of 'primal perception' – as Aldous Huxley noted when he took mescalin; he quoted Blake's statement: 'If the doors of perception were cleansed, every thing would appear to man as it is, infinite.' So cleansing the 'doors of perception' is basically a matter of brain physiology.

In the mid-sixties I began reading books on the brain; one result was a novel called *The Philosopher's Stone*, in which I suggest that the secret of primal perception may lie in the pre-frontal cortex. But it was more than ten years later that I came upon a crucial piece of research that threw a new light on the whole question. The result was revelatory, and requires a chapter to itself.

# TWO

# The Riddle of the 'Two Selves'

FOR SOME REASON that no physiologist yet understands, human beings have two brains. Or rather, the brain they possess is 'double' – almost as if a mirror had been placed down the middle, so that one half reflects the other. We seem to have two hearing centres, two visual centres, two muscle-control centres, even two memories. Why this should be so is baffling – one guess being that one of the brains is a 'spare' in case the other gets damaged. What seems even odder is that the left half of the brain controls the right side of the body, and vice versa.

From our point of view, the most interesting part of the brain is the bit at the top – the cerebral cortex. This is the most specifically human part; it has developed at an incredible speed over the past million or so years – so fast (in geological time) that some scientists like to speak of 'the brain explosion'.

If you could lift off the top of the skull and look down on the cerebral cortex, you would see something resembling a walnut, with two wrinkled halves. The bridge between them is a mass of nerve fibres called the *corpus callosum* or commissure.

This mass of millions of nerve fibres is obviously important. Which is why brain specialists were puzzled when they came across freaks who possessed no commissure, and appeared to function perfectly well without it. In the 1930s, brain surgeons wondered if they could prevent epileptic attacks by severing the *corpus callosum*, and so preventing the spread of the 'electrical storm' from one hemisphere to the other. They tried severing the commissure in monkeys and it seemed to do no harm. So they tried it on epileptic patients, and it seemed to work. The fits were greatly reduced – and the patient seemed much the same as before. One scientist remarked ironically that the only purpose of the commissure appeared to be to transmit epileptic seizures. Another suggested that it might be to prevent the brain from sagging in the middle.

In 1950, Roger W. Sperry, of the University of Chicago (and later of Cal Tech) began investigating the problem. He discovered that severing the commissure appeared to have no noticeable effect on cats and monkeys. But it *would* prevent one half of the brain learning what the other half knew. So if a cat was taught some trick with one eye covered up, and then asked to do it with the other eye covered, it was baffled. It could even be taught two different solutions to the same problem (say, pressing a lever to get food) with each side of the brain. There could be no doubt about it; we literally have two brains.

Sperry and his associate Michael Gazzaniga then studied a human patient whose brain had been split to prevent epileptic attacks. He seemed to be perfectly normal, except for one oddity – which they expected anyway. He could read with his right eye, but not with his left.* It had been known since the nineteenth century that, in human beings, the two halves of the brain seem to have different functions: 'right for recognition, left for language'. People who had damage to the right cerebral hemisphere were unable to recognise simple patterns, or enjoy music, but they could still speak normally. People with left-brain damage were able to recognise patterns, but their speech was impaired. Obviously, then, the left deals with language, and you would expect a split-brain patient to be unable to read with his right eye (connected, remember, to the opposite side of the brain). Sperry's patient was also

* In the following pages I shall speak of the right and left eyes; this is for purposes of simplification. What is actually involved is the right and left *visual fields*. One half of each eye is connected to the left-brain, one half to the right. So in visual experiments with split-brain patients, the patient is asked to keep his eyes focused on one field or the other. This makes no difference to the following exposition.

unable to write anything meaningful (i.e. complicated) with his left hand.

They noticed another oddity. If the patient bumped into something with his left side, he did not notice. And the implications here were very odd indeed. Not only did the split-brain operation give the patient *two separate minds*; it also seemed to restrict his identity, or ego, to the left side. When they placed an object in his left hand, and asked him what he was holding, he had no idea. Further experiments underlined the point. If a split-brain patient is shown two different symbols – say a circle and a square – with each eye, and is asked to say what he has just seen, he replies 'A square'. Asked to draw with his left hand what he has seen, and he draws a circle. Asked what he has just drawn, he replies: 'A square'. And when one split-brain patient was shown a picture of a nude male with the right-brain, she blushed; asked why she was blushing, she replied truthfully: 'I don't know.'

The implications are clearly staggering. The person you call 'you' lives in the left side of your brain. And a few centimetres away there is another person, a completely independent identity. Where language is concerned, this other person is almost an imbecile. In other respects, he is more competent than the inhabitant of the left-brain; for example, he can make a far more accurate perspective drawing of a house. In effect, the left-brain person is a scientist, the right-brain an artist.

These, then, are the basic facts about the two halves of the brain. It seems ironical that it should have taken me until 1978 to discover them (in Robert Ornstein's *Psychology of Consciousness* and Julian Jaynes's *Origin of Consciousness in the Breakdown of the Bicameral Mind* – an important book of which I shall have more to say later). I started taking *The Scientific American* in January 1964, and that particular issue contains Sperry's original classic article on 'The Great Cerebral Commissure'. Obviously, I didn't read it closely enough.

Now this realisation that 'I' live in the left half of the brain offered a solution to a problem that had bothered me for some time – in fact, ever since I had made a programme about a case of poltergeist activity for BBC television. Poltergeists are, as everyone knows, the knockabout comedians of the spirit world; they cause loud noises and strange events – like objects flying across the room. In the late nineteenth century, it became obvious to psychical researchers that poltergeists are not disembodied spirits; they are somehow caused by a mentally disturbed individual, usually an adolescent. (This, of course, is no final proof that a disembodied spirit is not involved – my own researches into the problem lead me to keep an open mind.) In the Rosenheim case – about which I made the programme – a girl named Anne-Marie Schaberl was the 'focus' of a series of poltergeist activities in a lawyer's office – oddly enough, many of them connected with electricity. The lights kept exploding, due to sudden tremendous surges of current. The phone bills were astronomical because someone – or something – was dialling the 'speaking clock' five or six times a minute for hours on end. But tests showed that even a practical joker could only dial 'tim' three times a minute, because it took twenty seconds to get through. Whatever was causing the trouble was getting straight through to the relays.

Anne-Marie was a country girl who hated working in a town, and in an office. Her father had been a harsh disciplinarian, so she had become accustomed to 'knuckling down' and swallowing her emotions. But apparently some other aspect of her being had other ideas, and set.out to wreck the office routine.

Professor Hans Bender, who investigated the case, told me that he had considerable difficulty convincing Anne-Marie that she was responsible, but that when she was finally convinced, she seemed secretly rather pleased. Moreover, said Bender, it is quite usual for children who cause poltergeist disturbances to be unaware that they are to blame; an investigator must be tactful in breaking the news, because some children become terrified.

How, I wondered, could a person be responsible for such amazing effects, and yet be totally unaware that she is causing them? Sperry's discovery provided the answer. We have two people living in our heads. And the finger seems to be pointing straight at the 'artist' who lives in the right-brain. That also seemed to make sense in that artists have a well-known dislike of mechanical, routine jobs – like work in a lawyer's office.

Another observation seemed to confirm this suspicion. I had become interested in dowsing ever since I discovered that I could use a divining rod. What intrigued me was that the rod seemed to twist in my hands without any co-operation from me; I was not in any way aware of causing it. But if it is the right-brain that is somehow responsible, then all would be explained. It would be my right-brain that would respond to the water, or the force in standing stones, and which would cause the contraction of the muscles that makes the dowsing rod react. An experiment performed by Gazzaniga seems to support this theory. The split-brain patient was asked to try to guess whether a red or green light had been flashed in his left eye. Since the right-brain cannot communicate with the left, the score should have been what you would expect from chance. In fact, the patient soon began to get it right each time. If he guessed wrongly, he would twitch or frown or shake his head, and change his guess: 'Red – oh no, I mean green.' The right-brain had overheard the wrong guess, and was communicating the correct one through the muscles – the equivalent of kicking him under the table or nudging him in the ribs.

But then, there is another interesting implication. Anne-Marie was not a split-brain patient; neither am I. So why should my right-brain need to communicate its observation that I am walking over an underground stream by making my muscles contract? Why can it simply not 'tell' me in the usual way – by making use of the bridge that exists?

The answer can be seen if we simply think about our experience of grasping our own intuitions. My consciousness is usually directed towards the outside world and its problems – and in coping with these problems I receive an enormous amount of help from the 'robot' (which seems to be situated in a 'lower' part of the brain called the cerebellum). I seldom 'look inside myself' and allow my feelings and intuitions to expand. When this occasionally happens – perhaps when I am listening to music or enjoying poetry – I have an odd feeling that my *sense of identity* has, so to speak, moved over towards the right. Half an hour before, I might have been biting my nails about some practical problems; now I look back on that tense, anxiety-ridden 'self' with patronising sympathy; he no longer seems to be 'me'.

Clearly, what I usually think of as 'me' is not me at all. But when I am trapped in that false 'me' of the left-brain, my communication with the intuitive 'me' is sadly limited. Which is why the right-brain needs to use a dowsing rod to communicate with me. We are *all* split-brain patients. If we weren't, composers would produce nothing but great symphonies and artists would paint nothing but masterpieces.

As soon as I begin thinking about this discovery that there are two 'me's' inside my skull, I see that it explains an enormous amount of my everyday experience. There is an intuitive 'me' and a critical 'me'. If, for example, I am thoroughly relaxed, and I am writing a letter, I actually enjoy the process of forming the letters, the sense of control. As soon as I become tense, my handwriting deteriorates; I lose that sense of control. Moreover, if someone comes and looks over my shoulder as I write, I become 'self-conscious' – or rather, left-brain-self-conscious – and again I write badly. This is the 'stage-fright' phenomenon, where my sheer anxiety to make a good impression leads to an excess of conscious control, and a reduction in efficiency. To do anything well, I need the co-operation of that 'other half'.

Again, I can study the interaction of the 'two me's' in my work as a writer. When I started writing, in my teens, it was because I was fascinated by the possibilities of self-expression as I saw them in writers I admired. But as soon as I began trying to turn my own intuitions and insights into words, I found I crushed them flat. Words seemed to be the enemy of insight, and their inability to reflect intuition seemed a mockery. But I went on writing, because there seemed nothing else to do; and gradually, I got better at it. There came the day when I looked at what I'd written, and it was still there. What I thought I'd said hadn't evaporated in the night. The left was slowly becoming more expert in turning the insights of the right into language. And sometimes, it did it so beautifully and economically that the right would get excited and say: 'Yes, yes, that's it!', and the left would feel delighted with the compliment and do its job even better, until the two were co-operating like two tennis players spurring one another on to play more and more brilliantly. This is obviously the state that artists call inspiration.

A little introspection also makes us aware that the left seems to be turned outward, towards the external world, while the right is turned inward, towards our inner-being. The business of the left is to 'cope' with everyday problems. The business of the right is to deal with our inner-states and feelings. And it also seems to be in charge of our energy supply. When I am feeling tense and overstretched, I only need to become *absorbed* in something to become aware that my energy-tanks are refilling. (T. E. Lawrence said: 'Happiness is absorption.') When I become absorbed in a book or a film, I say it 'takes me out of myself' – meaning literally that. It allows my centre of personal identity to move towards the right, away from this left-brain tyrant who would like to drive me like a galley slave. And soon that inner-spring of energy is brimming over with a sense of strength and relaxation.

The rule seems to be that if we need support and help, we need to ask for it by turning towards that 'other self' in the right-brain. Wordsworth's 'Intimations of Immortality' Ode shows the process in action. The poet feels depressed and jaded, and reflects gloomily upon his decreasing capacity for poetic inspiration. But the actual process of turning these insights into words makes him aware that things are not quite as bad as he thought, and he ends by writing confidently about a returning feeling of strength and optimism. The same process also explains why people who have suffered great personal loss often gain religious faith in exchange; the misery causes them to turn inward; the right responds with comfort and inspiration. The left-brain self becomes aware that it is not alone, and believes it has found God. Possibly it has; but it has certainly found its 'silent partner' who lives only a few centimetres away; and this, in its way, is just as great a discovery.

All this brings us, I think, a great deal closer to understanding that 'other mode' of consciousness. It is a type of consciousness with a great deal more of the right-brain in it than usual. Most of us achieve a certain practical balance between right and left for everyday purposes; and since one day is very much like another, we end by taking this balance for granted as a permanent and necessary state of affairs. It is nothing of the sort. A change of scenery, a change in our way of life, a new challenge, causes the right to improve our daily allowance of energy; and suddenly we feel renewed and reborn.

Then what is the secret of persuading the right to grant us more energy? For obviously, if we can discover this, we have discovered the secret of the 'other mode' – and probably the secret of human evolution.


At the time I first stumbled upon these discoveries about the right and left, I was engaged in writing a biography of Wilhelm Reich. Reich was, of course, a Freudian, and believed, like Freud, that all neurosis is sexual in origin. In tracing the sexual theory back to its origin, I discovered how Freud came to hold his peculiarly pessimistic views on the unconscious mind. Freud made his 'discovery of the unconscious' as a result of working with Charcot at the Salpétrière in Paris. Charcot had rediscovered the phenomena of hypnosis – originally observed by the Marquis de Puységur, a pupil of Mesmer, in the previous century. Mesmer aroused immense hostility amongst his medical colleagues and was forced to flee from Paris. Orthodox medicine was victorious, and during the nineteenth century, Mesmerism was regarded as another term for charlatanism. Hypnosis shared its fate – until it was given a new lease of life by Charcot, who noticed that it could produce a kind of artificial hysteria. Mental illnesses seem to occur in epidemics; and in the late nineteenth century, the chief mental illness was hysteria. Patients would suffer from hysterical paralysis, hysterical blindness and deafness, even hysterical pregnancy, in which the stomach would enlarge and the body exhibit all the normal symptoms of pregnancy. Charcot noticed that he could produce the same hysterical symptoms through hypnosis – and also, of course, undo them. His hysterical subjects could be made to have violent fits, to become paralysed, and to exhibit strength far beyond the normal – one of the favourite tricks of hypnotists was to tell a person that he had become as stiff as a board, then make him lie across two chairs – with his head on one, his feet on the other – while another person stood on his stomach, which remained unyielding. A hysterical patient could be made to produce 'stigmata' on his hands and feet, like the saints. He could be told that he was about to be touched with a red hot poker, and a blister would form where the hypnotist had touched him lightly with a finger. But if told that he would not bleed when a needle was driven into his arm, he would somehow obey the order, and the blood would refuse to flow.

Freud instantly saw that if there is a part of the mind that can perform these remarkable feats while the conscious mind is asleep, then it must be far more powerful than ordinary consciousness. He labelled it 'the unconscious'. But, being naturally a romantic pessimist by temperament, he also leapt to the conclusion that the unconscious is the real master. The conscious mind thinks it is in control when it is really a mere puppet in the hands of a force far greater than itself. And the mainspring of the unconscious mind is the sexual urge – a discovery Freud made as a result of the observations made by his friend Breuer upon a patient called Bertha Pappenheim. In her hysterical states, Bertha writhed her hips about as if in sexual intercourse or labour – which convinced Freud that her problems were basically sexual, but that it was her conscious repression of her sexual urge that caused the neurosis. (He was mistaken; her problems were due to nervous exhaustion and misery after watching her father die slowly of cancer.) So, according to Freud, neurosis was due to the festering of sexual 'splinters' in the unconscious mind.

Freud's mistake lay in his assumption that, because the unconscious mind is so much more powerful than the conscious, it must be the real master. The ship is far more powerful than the captain; but the captain decides which way it will go; an elephant is more powerful than the boy who sits on its head; but the boy gives the orders.

It was clear to me that the real cause of neurosis is the conflict between the left- and right-brain 'egos'. The left ego is the master of consciousness; the right is master of the unconscious. And the relation between the two is not unlike the relation between Laurel and Hardy in the old movies. Ollie is the left-brain, the boss. Stan takes his cues from Ollie. When Ollie is in a good mood, Stan is delighted. When Ollie is depressed, Stan is plunged into the depths of gloom. Stan is inclined to *over-react*.

When Ollie wakes up on a wet Monday morning, he thinks: 'Damn, it's raining, and I've got a particularly dreary day in front of me . . .' Stan overhears this and sinks into depression. And – since he controls the energy supply – Ollie has that 'sinking feeling', and feels drained of energy. This makes him feel worse than ever. As he walks out of the gate he bumps into a man who tells him to look where he's going, then trips over a crack in the pavement, then misses a bus just as he arrives at the stop, and thinks: 'This is going to be one of those days . . .' And again, Stan overhears, and feels worse than ever. And once more, Ollie feels that sinking feeling. By the end of the day, he may be feeling suicidal – not because things have been really bad, but because of a continual 'negative feedback' of gloom between the right and left.

Consider, on the other hand, what happens to a child on Christmas Day. He wakes up full of pleasurable anticipation; Stan instantly sends up a flood of energy. When he goes downstairs, everything reinforces the feeling of delight – Christmas carols on the radio, the Christmas tree with its lights, the smell of mince pies in the oven. Each new stimulus causes a new rush of delight; each new rush of delight deepens the feeling that 'all is well', and that the world is a wonderful and exciting place after all. Suddenly, he is in the 'other mode' of consciousness; the feeling that all is well has produced a new level of trust and relaxation. He is no longer inclined to wince, as if expecting a blow; the left-brain tyrant is as utterly relaxed as if he was hypnotised.

Considerations like these make it clear that our chief problem is 'generalised hypertension', a basic feeling of mistrust about the world. The 'other mode' depends upon a degree of communication between the two halves, and this in turn depends upon 'positive feedback'. If I experience some enormous relief, as some appalling threat is removed, Ollie gives a sigh of contentment, and Stan reacts by sending up a wave of relief. And suddenly, Ollie is seeing things in a completely new way – grass looks greener, everything is somehow 'more interesting'.

What precisely happens in such moments? The first thing to note is that when we experience relief, we feel we can *afford* to relax. When I step into a hot bath at the end of a hard day's work, or open a bottle of wine as I prepare to watch the news, I tell myself, as it were: 'You deserve this.' But this concept of 'affording' indicates that we think of our energies in much the same way we think of our bank accounts: as something quite definite and *limited*. This is why I get annoyed if I am trying to change the plug on the electric kettle and the phone rings; I feel this is a tiresome attempt to divert my energies when I need them all for the task in hand. I have *narrowed down* my attention, and I feel that anything that tries to widen it is a nuisance.

Conversely, when I experience relief because some problem has vanished, I allow my field of awareness to widen. And it is this widening that brings the 'peak experience'. Maslow's young mother was feeling quite cheerful as she watched her family eating breakfast, but her attention was fixed on the task in hand – watching to see the baby didn't knock its cereal on the floor. The beam of sunlight triggered a relaxation response, a widening. And the widening brought the peak experience.

It begins to look as if we have discovered the basic mechanism of the peak experience. But there is still an important question to answer. If 'narrowing' somehow prevents the peak experience, why do we do it? Of course, we all know that 'narrowing' makes us more efficient; I shall make a better job of changing the plug if I give it my full attention. But we seem to habitually overdo it.

Here again, we are dealing with the subject of hysteria. At the same time that Charcot was studying hypnosis in Paris, his younger contemporary Pierre Janet was studying the effects of hysteria. He was particularly fascinated by a rather odd manifestation of hysteria called multiple personality. In such cases, the patient has split into two or more people – completely different individuals, who take it in turns to occupy the body, just as different drivers might take over a hire-car. A typical case was reported by the psychologist Cyril Burt.* In 1917, a foreman named Naylor was accused by two workmates of seducing their wives: both had received letters, couched in filthy language, describing Naylor as a philanderer. Naylor himself had received similar letters; so had his employer and the local vicar. Oddly enough, they were signed with the name of his only daughter, May. And May was a quiet, well-behaved girl who obviously knew nothing about them. Burt was asked to investigate. He discovered that the nine-year-old girl was a model pupil at school, of superior intellectual ability, and with no record of practical joking. Her handwriting was neat, and completely unlike that of the anonymous letters. Yet when she told Burt that her favourite flower was the lily of the valley because it was so white and pure, Burt began to wonder if this was not too much of a good thing. He hypnotised the girl, and a completely different character emerged – a coarse, vengeful, foul-mouthed child who detested her father as much as the 'other May' loved him. May was, in fact, a Jekyll and Hyde. Under Burt's treatment, she was finally 'cured'.

* *The Young Delinquent*, University of London Press, 1931, pp. 384–91. Oddly enough, Burt does not mention that May was a case of multiple personality, probably because the concept was out of favour in 1931.

The most striking thing about this case is its resemblance to the Anne-Marie poltergeist case. May Naylor wrote obscene letters; Anne-Marie made electric lights explode – both quite 'unknowingly'. Could that mean that the delinquent May was simply a manifestation of her own right-brain? Hardly; for the right-brain differs from the left simply in its basic activities: it is concerned with over-all patterns and meanings rather than with down-to-earth problems. Besides, in some cases of multiple personality, there have been literally dozens of 'other selves', all of them quite distinct. Clearly, we cannot blame the right-brain for May's misbehaviour. This is a more complicated problem.

Janet noticed an interesting thing about hysterics: that in many respects, they behaved just like multiple personalities. One of his patients, for example, was a hysterical woman who had worried herself into such a state of anxiety that she stared straight in front of her, concentrating upon some vaguely defined worry. In order to attract her attention, Janet had to speak loudly in her ear. But he discovered that if he said in a quiet voice: 'Raise your right arm', she would obey. If he then asked her loudly: 'Why have you got your right arm in the air?', the woman would looked amazed; she had no memory of raising it. Her conscious 'self' had narrowed down, but 'unconscious' areas of her personality were still accessible. She had, in effect, become two people. Her neurotic anxiety made her suppress her 'wider self'. And multiple personalities appear to do just this. Most of them have had traumatic childhoods, and they face life with extreme caution and mistrust. Some severe shock then causes them to 'split' into two different people; the suppressed part gets its own back by taking over the body. (And the original personality – the one suffering from anxiety – usually has no memory of what happens during these periods of 'takeover'.)

So in the case of May Naylor, it seems likely that the 'good May' was over-anxious to please, and that she suppressed all natural naughtiness in order to win the favour of her parents and teachers. Her own anxiety about her 'naughty' impulses had the effect of amplifying them – what Viktor

Frankl calls 'the law of reverse effort' (i.e. a stammerer who tries hard not to stammer becomes worse than ever) – until she was suppressing a virtual juvenile delinquent. This delinquent, robbed of any form of self-expression, finally became strong enough to take over May's body, and write the obscene letters about her father.

It is not an easy concept to grasp – the notion that 'narrowing' our awareness can turn us into more than one person. But it does seem to be so. And it provides a clue to what is wrong with most of us. We are all 'partial personalities'; we are all 'hysterics'. And this is an inevitable consequence of the sheer complexity of human life. Imagine a woman making an enormous patchwork quilt; it is so big that she seldom sees the whole thing. As she works, she is only aware of a fairly small part of it. It is the same with any 'cumulative' activity. When I first started collecting gramophone records, it was easy to 'know' my collection; but as it gradually grew bigger, I had to keep a catalogue. And now, if I want to know if I have a particular recording of a Mahler symphony, I have to look in my catalogue, instead of instantly being able to recall the record. The size of my collection means I can only 'know' a small portion at a time.

In the same way, we spend our lives accumulating new experiences. My brain stores all these experiences; and the neurologist Wilder Penfield discovered that if he touched a part of the temporal cortex of the brain with an electric probe during an operation, the patient (who was conscious) recalled experiences that took place years ago in the utmost detail, exactly as if re-living them. But for practical purposes, most of our experiences are lost. And my personality, unlike my record collection, has never been catalogued. So whole vast areas of my being are packed away – on microfilm, as it were.

The fascinating implication is that if I could somehow 'spread out' my personality – as the woman can spread out her patchwork quilt – I would be amazed to discover that I am far 'bigger' than I had ever suspected. Or, to put it plainly, more 'godlike'. Moreover, those moods of 'wider consciousness' – the 'other mode' – allow me a glimpse of the sheer size

of the quilt. Hermann Hesse described such a moment in
*Steppenwolf*, where the hero is in bed with a pretty girl:

'For moments together my heart stood still between
delight and sorrow to find how rich was the gallery of my life,
and how thronged the soul of the wretched Steppenwolf with
high eternal stars and constellations . . .'

Yeats was obviously speaking of the same experience
when he wrote in *Under Ben Bulben*:

> Know that when all words are said
> And a man is fighting mad,
> Something drops from eyes long blind,
> He completes his partial mind,
> For an instant stands at ease,
> Laughs aloud, his heart at peace . . .

Here the important phrase is 'he completes his partial
mind'. Yeats's preoccupation with moon-imagery leads one to
suspect that he was thinking of the 'completed mind' as
something like the full moon, and the 'partial mind' – the
everyday self – as the moon in its last quarter. And this
symbol provides a useful image of the human psyche, with
the 'everyday self' as the last quarter:

Janet's hysterical patient was a very thin slice indeed,
hardly more than a sliver. (Oddly enough, such patients often

suffer from 'tunnel vision', a narrowing of the visual field.)
But her 'wider self' was still there:

But then, if we are all, in some respect, hysterical
patients, then the above diagram applies to all of us. Outside
the 'everyday self' there is a kind of grey, penumbral area of
the wider-self. I experience this wider-self whenever some
interesting challenge makes me feel 'more alive'. Conversely,
whenever I am bored and tired, the everyday-self contracts,
and the penumbral area becomes correspondingly bigger.
Most of us, even in our moments of greatest anxiety, never
become as narrow as Janet's patient.

Now in the 'other mode' of consciousness, the whole
personality seems to expand; the quarter moon turns into
something closer to a half. This is more than the usual feeling
of increased 'interest' or vitality, or even T. E. Lawrence's
'absorption'. When we are happy, we still see the world in
more or less the same way as when we are unhappy or merely
indifferent. We just seem to see *more* of it; the change is
quantitative. In the 'other mode', the change seems to be
qualitative; we have an odd sense of revelation or insight, a
desire to snap our fingers and say: 'Of *course!*' Of course *what?*
Even if we can manage to cling on to some fragments of that
insight, it seems impossible to express. And the reason it is so
hard to express is that we see that 'everyday consciousness' is
somehow based upon a set of *false assumptions*, so that we
would have to start by explaining what is wrong with these

assumptions. And this sets the solution of the problem back another pace. . . .

Still, let us make the attempt. To begin with, the 'false assumption' lies in the fact that I take it for granted that 'I' am the quarter-moon. My everyday sense of identity usually seems quite solid and secure; when mixing with other people, I am aware that they see me as a definite person; and *I* feel myself to be a definite person. When I experience ordinary happiness, I am still a definite person – but a happy one. But as soon as I experience the 'other mode', my mind seems to perform a kind of conjuring trick that makes me gape with astonishment. The boundaries of my everyday self seem to dissolve, and I turn into 'something bigger'. It is almost as if the blood was returning into an arm or leg that had 'gone to sleep' because I had been lying on it. Moreover, there is an intuition that this 'new self' is not sharply defined by 'identity', like my everyday self. It seems to stretch into the distance. This sense of boundlessness is so foreign to our everyday experience that it produces a sensation of paradox. This is why Steppenwolf can talk about himself as 'the wretched Steppenwolf', as if he was speaking of another person. What seems even more paradoxical is that this new sense of 'self' is stronger than the everyday identity, even though it has no boundaries to define it.

But at least, we can now begin to understand precisely why the 'everyday self' is a kind of hysteric. In 'stage fright', the left-brain is gripped by mistrust and a sense of inadequacy. It is rather as if a man who had to make a speech suddenly began to worry about whether his mouth would open and close, and tried to do it with his fingers. Obviously, he would speak badly. In effect, a man suffering from over-anxiety is clutching his own windpipe, and wondering why he feels suffocated. We can perfectly well understand what is wrong with such a person – recognise that he is over-reacting, and that he needs to stop indulging his hysteria. But we think of ourselves as 'normal' and balanced. We think of our own left-brain reactions to the world as sensible and responsible. So it is difficult to grasp that, even in the most sensible person, there is still a kind of hysteria which somehow keeps him trapped and confused. In his important essay 'The Energies of Man', William James puts his finger on the problem: 'Most of us feel as if a sort of cloud weighed upon us, keeping us below our highest notch in discernment. Compared to what we ought to be, we are only half awake.' James also compares us to hysterics: 'In every conceivable way [my] life is contracted like the field of vision of an hysteric subject – but with less excuse, for the poor hysteric is diseased, while in the rest of us, it is only an inveterate *habit* – the habit of inferiority to our full self – that is bad.'

James was not aware that the right and left sides of the brain contain two different people, so he lacked an important clue for understanding how this 'hysteria' comes about. As to the question of how to remedy the situation, he had no very useful ideas. Speaking of certain people who seem less 'inferior to their full self' than the rest of us, he says: 'Either some unusual stimulus fills them with emotional excitement, or some unusual idea of necessity induces them to make an extra effort of will. *Excitements, ideas, and efforts*, in a word, are what carry us over the dam.'

This is a worthwhile insight, but it simply takes us back to the position of 'the Outsider', who is always looking for extreme or violent methods for escaping from his sense of suffocation. He may preach revolution, he may take drugs, he may subject himself to extreme physical hardships 'so that he might feel the life within him more intensely' (as Shaw's Shotover puts it); he may even, like Dostoevsky's Raskolnikov, commit murder. But all these methods involve the same assumption: that the answer lies 'out there', in the physical world. We have seen, beyond all shadow of doubt, that the answer lies 'inside' – in that other self who inhabits the right-brain.

But this analysis has answered another of the major questions of 'the Outsider'. He experiences the moment of intensity, of insight, of 'absurd good news', and then wonders whether it was all an illusion. Our knowledge of the mechanisms involved enables us to state authoritatively that it is not an illusion. The business of the right-brain is pattern-recognition, the 'bird's-eye view'. The left-brain is confined to the worm's-eye view. Where over-all patterns and meanings are concerned, a bird's-eye view undoubtedly provides a truer picture than the worm's. So we conclude that the sense of 'absurd good news', the feeling that 'all is well', *is* justified.

The next problem is how to *bring home* this insight to the everyday self, to the left-brain ego. But first of all, we need to look more closely into the curious powers of the right-brain.

It should be mentioned that the psychologist Stan Gooch remains convinced that the notion of 'two selves' living in the right- and left-brains is all a mistake. In *Total Man* (1972), Gooch committed himself to the view that the seat of the unconscious is the cerebellum – the part of the 'old brain' directly below the cerebral hemispheres. (The pineal gland was once an eye – or possibly two eyes – in the top of the cerebellum.) Recently, he has described cases of 'hemispherectomy' – total removal of the left-brain, usually to cure cancer – in which the patient (even a man of forty-seven) has slowly regained some slight ability to speak. According to the view of Sperry and Ornstein, total removal of the left hemisphere should cause a kind of idiocy, 'nobody at home' (since the 'I' lives in the left).

But these controversies are irrelevant to the present argument. If Gooch is right, then the 'I' lives in the cerebral hemispheres – both of them – and the 'other I' in the cerebellum. The central point – that we are two people – remains unchanged. My own view is that both Gooch and Ornstein are partly right, and that the right hemisphere is, so to speak, the 'antechamber' of the unconscious mind, whose 'seat' may lie elsewhere in the brain, even possibly extending to the body.

# THREE

# More Mysteries

ON FEBRUARY 21, 1977, a forty-eight-year-old Philippino woman named Teresita Basa was murdered in her apartment in Chicago; she had been stabbed several times, and an attempt had been made to burn her body. The police were unable to find any important clues, although the motive seems to have been robbery. Five months later, in July, Dr Jose Chua and his wife Remibias – also from the Philippines – were sitting in their apartment in Evanston when Mrs Chua got up abruptly and walked into the bedroom. The doctor followed her, and found her lying in a trance-like state on the bed. When he asked her what was wrong, a strange voice issued from her mouth saying, in Tagalog (the language of the Philippines): 'I am Teresita Basa.' She went on to say that she had been murdered by a fellow employee at the Edgewater Hospital, a black named Allan Showery. He had, she said, killed her and stolen some jewellery.

When Mrs Chua woke up, she remembered nothing of what had happened; apparently she had, quite spontaneously, become a 'medium'. A few days later, it happened again. This time, Dr Chua told the 'spirit' that the police would need evidence; it replied that Showery still had some of the stolen jewellery in his possession, and that her pearl cocktail ring was now on the finger of Showery's common law wife. Still the Chuas found themselves unable to go to the police. But when the 'spirit' manifested itself a third time, they apparently decided that it would be less trouble to do what it asked. As a result, the Chicago police questioned them, then called on Allan Showery. They found the jewellery, just as the 'voice' had said, and his common law wife was wearing the cocktail ring. Under questioning, Showery admitted that he had gone into Miss Basa's apartment – the woman had been a Manila socialite before coming to America, hence the jewellery – and murdered her, then taken the jewellery.

There is, admittedly, room for a grain of doubt about the truth of this story. Mrs Chua worked in the same hospital as the dead woman, and had actually left just before her 'possession', saying that she was afraid of Showery. She could have suspected him, and used this method of telling the police. But that hardly makes sense; all she had to do was to give them an anonymous tip-off – why involve her husband in the incredible story about the 'voice'?

The story interests me, not because it seems to provide evidence for life-after-death, but because it indicates something that strikes me as equally intriguing: that the human body can be 'taken over' by other personalities, who use it in the same way that successive drivers use a hire-car. Such a view seems, in a way, contrary to experience because we somehow take it for granted that the personality and the body are very closely involved. I recall reading *Frankenstein* as a child, and suddenly being struck by this paradox of the 'self'. Suppose Victor Frankenstein had removed the monster's arms and replaced them with new ones; would it still be the same monster? Obviously yes. But he could go on removing parts and changing them for others until he had enough spare parts to make another monster; at what point, precisely, would it cease to be 'the same monster' and become another one?

In his book *The Shape of Minds to Come*, Professor John Taylor states the standard view of personality: '. . . we recognise personality as a summation of the different contributions to behaviour from the various control units of the brain.' That seems to make sense. Yet cases like that of Teresita Basa suggest otherwise. So do many cases that seem to suggest 'reincarnation'. In *Mysteries* I mention the case of Jasbir Lal, a three-year-old Hindu boy who apparently 'died' of smallpox. Fortunately, his father decided to wait until the next day before burying him; by morning, the child had

awakened again. But as he slowly recovered, his family
became aware that he seemed to be a different personality.
And he said as much. He claimed to be the son of a Brahmin
of another village, and at first declined to eat with the family,
who were of a lower caste. A few years later, the child
'recognised' a Brahmin lady who was visiting his village,
claiming she was his aunt. This lady confirmed what the child
had said: that at the time he had 'died' of smallpox, a young
man named Sobha Ram had also died in Vehedi village, due to
a fall from a cart. (In fact, the child insisted Sobha Ram had
died from poison, but this never seems to have been confirmed.) Taken to Vehedi under supervision, Jasbir was able
to lead the investigators – by a complicated route – to Sobha
Ram's house, and he demonstrated a detailed knowledge of
the family and its affairs. The case is cited by Dr Ian
Stevenson (in *Twenty Cases Suggestive of Reincarnation*), who
agrees that it looks very much like a proven case of reincarnation. But Sobha Ram died when Jasbir was three. . . .

In 1877, there occurred in America a case that has some
striking resemblances to that of Jasbir. On July 11, a thirteen-
year-old girl named Lurancy Verrum, who lived in Watseka,
Illinois, had a fit, and was unconscious for five hours. It
happened again the next day; but while lying 'unconscious',
she went on speaking, declaring she was in heaven, and could
see a little brother and sister who had died. As similar trances
kept recurring, the family concluded she was mentally
disturbed, and thought of sending her into a mental home.
However, at this point, a Mr and Mrs Asa Roff – friends of the
family – intervened. Their daughter Mary, who had been
dead twelve years, had behaved in a similar manner, and they
persuaded the Verrums to allow them to bring along a friend,
Dr E. W. Stevens. On the day Stevens was introduced to
Lurancy, the girl was in a savage mood; but she talked to the
doctor, and stated at one point that she was an old woman
named Katrina Hogan, and then that she was a man named
Willie Canning. After another 'fit', Stevens calmed her with
hypnosis; then the girl declared that she was being possessed
by evil spirits. Stevens, who knew something about spiritual-

ism, suggested that she needed a 'guide' or control, and Lurancy agreed. She said that someone called Mary Roff had offered to help her. Mrs Roff, who was present, said this would be an excellent idea. . . .

The next day, Lurancy was no longer 'herself', but Mary Roff. She recognised none of her family, but asked to go 'home' to the Roffs' house. (Mary had died at the age of eighteen in 1865.) As Mrs Roff and one of her married daughters approached the Verrum home, Lurancy, who was looking out of the window, said excitedly: 'There's my ma and sister Nervie.' She wept for joy when they came into the house. A few days later, the Verrums allowed 'Mary' to go home to the Roffs' house. She showed the same precise, detailed knowledge of the Roff family that Jasbir showed of Sobha Ram's. Asked how long she could stay, she replied that 'the angels' had given her until May. And on May 21, Mary announced that she would have to leave 'Rancy's' body at eleven o'clock. Mary took tender leave of all her family, then returned to the Roff home. On the way, she became Lurancy again. And from then on, Lurancy was a perfectly normal girl.

Now obviously, cases like these suggest very strongly that 'personality' can survive bodily death. In which case, it would seem possible that cases of multiple personality are really cases of 'possession'. Yet while this is a hypothesis that should not be totally dismissed, it would leave us with just as many problems as before. For the real mystery here is: what precisely *is* a 'personality'? Is each person really an 'individual' – an indivisible unity? We know this is not so; we react differently in different situations, and it is quite easy to imagine the same person behaving like totally different people in different situations. But this, we say, is merely a question of different 'aspects' of the same personality. But then, in cases of multiple personality, it looks as if different sets of 'aspects' have come together to form totally different personalities. Many people seem so limited and boring that it is quite easy to believe that they have half a dozen other personalities hidden away in some recess of the mind. In short, personality seems to be like a suit of clothes; and it is possible for everyone to possess any number.

Besides, my personality seems to be closely connected with my conscious-self. If someone asks you whether you remembered to pass on a message, you may reply: 'No, it didn't come into my head.' Yet it *was* in your head – somewhere. It just didn't happen to emerge into the *centre* of consciousness. And in that gigantic storehouse of memories and experiences inside my head, there must be material for hundreds of 'personalities'. By 'the' personality, we mean only the one in the centre of consciousness.

A case history will underline the point. In the year that Lurancy Verrum began having fits, a fourteen-year-old boy named Louis Vivé was attacked by a viper and severely traumatised. Vivé was a neglected child who had been in a reformatory since he was ten; he was quiet and obedient. But after the shock, he began having fits, and was sent to the asylum at Bonneval. One day, he had a 'hysterico-epileptic attack' which lasted fifteen hours; when he recovered, he was a different person. To begin with, he no longer suffered from hysterical hemiplegia (paralysis of one side of the body). He had no memory of anything that had happened since the viper attack. And he was violent, dishonest, and generally badly behaved. This new 'delinquent' self would alternate with the former, well-behaved Louis Vivé, who suffered from paralysis.

After a period in the marines, and a conviction for theft, Vivé was sent to the asylum at Rochefort, where three doctors became intrigued by his case of hysterical hemiplegia. By this time, the 'bad' character was present most of the time. He was paralysed down the right side, and his speech was halting and poor. But in spite of this, he was given to delivering violent harangues 'with a monkey-like impudence' on atheism and the need for violent revolution.

The doctors believed that hysterical hemiplegia could be transferred from one side to the other by various metals. Vivé responded to steel, which transferred the hemiplegia from one side to the other. And there was an instant change of character;

Vivé was again a quiet, well-behaved person, who remembered nothing of his career as a violent radical and criminal.

We, of course, have a clue that was unknown to Vivé's doctors: that when his right side was paralysed, his left-brain was affected – hence the poor speech. So the 'person' who expressed himself in the violent speeches was Vivé's 'right-brain self'. The steel caused the paralysis to reverse, and the left-brain Vivé returned.

This is not to say – obviously – that the revolutionary Vivé was a totally right-brain being, since he was able to express himself in speech. Presumably both personalities made use of both sides of the brain. But the 'well-behaved' Vivé was oriented to the left, and the badly behaved Vivé to the right.

Now oddly enough, this seems to be a recurring pattern in such cases. One of the most fully documented is that of Christine Beauchamp, described around the turn of the century by Dr Morton Prince in his book *The Dissociation of a Personality*.* Christine, the primary personality, was quiet and undemonstrative. Like Vivé, she had had a difficult time in late childhood. A severe psychological shock brought on a period of depression and general exhaustion. Under hypnosis, another personality emerged, who called herself Sally. Sally's speech was impaired – she stuttered. But she was in every way livelier and healthier than Christine. Christine was unaware of Sally's existence, but Sally knew everything that went on in Christine's mind. When Christine was 'low', Sally could take over the body. And the personalities of the two were so different that Prince could tell at a glance whether it was Sally or Christine 'in the body'. On one occasion, Christine was about to take a trip to Europe for her health; Prince called at the hospital to enquire about her, and was surprised to hear that she was in the best of health and spirits. Entering the room, he instantly saw why; Sally had taken over, determined that Christine's poor health should not deprive her of a holiday in Europe. Prince says: 'As I walked into the room I was astonished to see not Miss Beauchamp but Sally, stuttering and merry as a

---

* More fully discussed in *Mysteries*, Part 2, Chap. 2.

grig.' In fact, the holiday kept Christine in such good spirits that Sally was unable to take over.

The case of 'Doris Fischer', described by Dr Walter Prince, has a similar pattern.* Doris was a quiet, timid child who was badly treated by her father. After a severe shock (all such cases seem to begin in the same way), her alter-ego 'Margaret' made her appearance. Margaret, like Sally Beauchamp, was cheerful, healthy and mischievous. Both were given to playing malicious tricks on the 'primary personality'. (Sally used to take long walks into the country, then abandon the body and leave the easily exhausted Christine to walk back.)

Now it is certainly tempting to see here the kind of self-division we all experience. I may feel too lethargic to go for a long walk, and force myself to do it 'against my will'. But the 'division' here is between my body, which feels tired, and my 'controlling ego', which feels that a walk would nevertheless be good for me. A rather more interesting form of 'division' occurs if I am not physically tired, but simply bored with the idea of a walk, so that the very thought rouses internal resistance. If I now force myself to go, I am aware of something much more like 'two selves' in conflict. The interesting point to note here is that if I force myself to walk until I feel I can no longer drag myself a step further, I can usually force myself through some kind of psychological 'barrier', and experience 'second wind'. Quite suddenly, the fatigue vanishes and I feel able to go on for miles. In 'The Energies of Man', William James reports that this used to be a favourite method of treating 'neurasthenic' patients suffering from permanent exhaustion; the doctor forces the patient to make immense efforts, which at first cause acute distress; then the distress suddenly vanishes and gives way to relief.

These different 'levels' of personality seem to bear no obvious resemblance to cases like that of Louis Vivé or Doris Fischer, where it seems to be a matter of completely different 'persons'. In her book on the case of 'Sybil' (who exhibited

* Also discussed in *Mysteries*, Part 2, Chap. 2.

sixteen different 'selves'), Flora Rheta Schreiber mentions that tests with an EEG machine (for measuring 'brainwaves') reveal that the different personalities in such cases often have different brain patterns. This seems impossible – as remarkable as the same person having several different sets of fingerprints. But no one supposes that a person who has just got 'second wind' has a different brain pattern. It is almost as if we could be 'divided' two ways – vertically or horizontally. A person like Louis Vivé seems to switch horizontally, as if the two 'persons' involved completely different interactions of the right- and left-brain. A neurasthenic patient who is 'bullied' into a more vital state seems to have moved vertically, as if climbing a ladder.

Yet the two systems, horizontal and vertical, are plainly connected. Why is it that all cases of multiple personality seem to begin with a shock? Presumably because the shock causes a sudden drop in vitality – a descent down several rungs of the 'ladder'. And this 'fall' allows the secondary personality to assume control.

The Victorian scientist Sir Francis Galton performed an experiment that demonstrates a controlled 'descent' of the ladder. He deliberately induced in himself a persecuted state of mind, walking through London and telling himself that everyone he met was a spy. It was alarmingly successful, so that when he passed a cab stand in Piccadilly, he had a feeling that all the horses were watching him. It took several hours for him to get back to normal, and even then, it was easy to slip back into his mild paranoia. Intrigued by this experiment, Professor Peter McKellar of New Zealand tried persuading friends in a restaurant that the waiter had something against them and was determined not to serve them; he records that he was surprised how easily he could induce a state of mild paranoia.*

McKellar also mentions an interesting experiment conducted by Dr E. A. Kaplan in which a hypnotised subject was told that his left hand would be insensitive to pain, while the

---

* *Mindsplit*, Dent and Co., 1979, p. 164.

right hand would be capable of automatic writing. When the left hand was pricked by a needle, the patient felt nothing, but the right hand wrote: 'Ouch, it hurts.' This certainly seems to reveal a sub-system of personality split off from the rest. Moreover, it is a sub-system which, like Vivé's, is associated with the right and left halves of the brain. But here again, we must beware of the assumption that the secondary personality 'is' the 'right-brain self'. William James performed an experiment in automatic writing; his subject was a college student. When the hand that was doing the writing was pricked, the student was unaware of it, although he reacted sharply if his left hand was pricked. But the right hand wrote: 'Don't you prick me any more.' Later, the student was asked to try automatic writing with the left hand, and was then asked how many times James had pricked his right hand; the left hand answered accurately 'Nineteen'. So the sub-personality that did the writing had use of both hands; presumably it also had the use of both sides of the brain.

Before we allow this subject to lead us farther afield, we need some further clarification of the respective roles of the right and left hemispheres.

To begin with, we must avoid falling into the obvious trap of regarding the right as a hero and the left as a villain. The error is more dangerous because it is not entirely without foundation. The 'left' *does* tend to behave like a nagging and self-opinionated housewife, obsessed with its own trivial purposes, continually imposing its own simplistic notions on the complexity of reality. For the past two centuries, poets and artists have been warning us against the rational intellect. Blake makes it the villain of his prophetic books (where he calls it Urizen). Wordsworth recognised that it was chiefly to blame for the 'shades of the prison house' that close around us as we grow up. T. E. Lawrence called the intellect his 'jailer', and said that the richness of physical reality is 'filtered and made typical' by thought.

It is also true that the states of mind William James called 'melting moods' occur when the left relaxes its neurotic vigilance. It happens when we sigh with relief, or when we are suddenly filled with delighted anticipation – perhaps when setting out on a holiday. But all this proves is that the left-brain in modern man has become too dominant for its own good: not that it should surrender its dominance to the right. If cases of secondary personality are anything to go by – May Naylor, Louis Vivé, Sally Beauchamp, Doris Fischer – 'surrender to the right' would be no solution at all. (Morton Prince remarks that secondary personalities are always inferior to the 'original self'.) Stan may be in many ways preferable to Ollie, but he is not cut out to be the leader and make the decisions. In the twentieth century, Hermann Hesse has been one of the few major writers to understand this; in *Glimpse into Chaos* (1919), he warns Europe against being taken over by a 'primeval, occult, Asiatic ideal' – an ideal he calls 'Russian man'. Russian man, he says, 'is not to be adequately described either as a "hysteric" or as a drunkard or criminal, or as a poet and holy man, but only as the simultaneous combination of all these characteristics'. Hesse is describing a 'right-brainer', a character not unlike the 'revolutionary' alter-ego of Louis Vivé.

This is a difficult point to grasp, since 'right-brain' moods – of relaxation and expansion – are so obviously desirable. They fill us with optimism and replenish our vital energies. Everything looks clearer and brighter; scents, colours, sounds, become richer, so that we have a sense of being almost overwhelmed by meanings that we usually overlook. And yet – oddly enough – we can easily grow tired of them. Like a hot bath, they leave us relaxed and refreshed – but who would want to spend twenty-four hours in a hot bath?

It is not easy to see why precisely this should be so. But this is because we spend most of our time in a state of meaning-starvation; so the idea of growing tired of too much 'meaning' seems as absurd as growing tired of food would seem to a starving man. The fact remains that a starving man grows tired of food once he is full up.

Meaning, like food, is not an end in itself. My body converts food into energy, and my mind converts meaning into purpose. Why? Because this seems to be the nature of the evolutionary drive. There is no point in being overwhelmed by meaning – like the mystics. Our task is to *pin it down*. When a scientist glimpses a new truth, he immediately sets about converting it into concepts and symbols. If he failed to do this because it was too big, too complex, he would only feel frustrated.

The fundamental human urge is not for happiness, but for control. A man who has spent his life in a state of misery may be glad enough for a few scraps of happiness; but the moment he becomes a little accustomed to happiness, he is seized with a desire to grasp its underlying principle, so that he can turn it on and off as he pleases. The romantic poets and artists of the nineteenth century had their glimpses of ecstasy and moments of vision; what made them so unhappy was their lack of control over them. After all, a vision is an insight, and an insight is something I ought to be able to recall at will. If a 'vision' comes and goes as it pleases, and I am unable to remember what it was about, then I am probably better off without it.

In short, insight is not enough. The two halves need to combine their functions. When this happens, the result is far greater than either could achieve individually. In *The Dam Busters*, Paul Brickhill describes how the planes that bombed the Moener dam maintained an exact height above the water; a powerful light was placed in the nose and tail of each aeroplane, so the two beams crossed at the necessary height. All the pilot had to do was to reach the height at which there was only one circle of light on the water instead of two, then release his bombs. In the same way, the faculties of the right and left hemispheres, of insight and logic, can be focused together at a single point. When this happens, the result is a *sense of actuality*, as if the mind had suddenly 'got the distance' between itself and the real world. For this sense of actuality I have suggested the term 'Faculty X'.

And it should be clear that the most important element in Faculty X is not the 'insight', but the discipline and control of the 'left-brain'. Gibbon has described how the inspiration for the *Decline and Fall* came to him as he sat among the ruins of the Capitol, listening to bare-foot friars singing vespers. It was his first visit to Rome, and no doubt the reality of the place brought that sense of insight, the feeling that *here* was the place that was the historical and religious centre of ancient Rome. But the insight would not have come if he had not first studied Roman history. An ignorant peasant would only have seen a lot of ruins. Gibbon *brought to a focus* his sense of the present and his knowledge of the past. And that knowledge – which had no doubt cost him a great deal of boredom and several beatings (he described his school as 'a cavern of fear and sorrow') – was the more important of the two elements.

It is true that we do not *need* this kind of knowledge to achieve Faculty X – Proust experienced it tasting a cake dipped in herb tea and tripping over a paving stone. No doubt Paris experienced Faculty X the first time Helen of Troy surrendered herself. But occasions like this are rare because our senses are dulled by habit. And when we become habit-bound, we cease even to try to bring the two 'beams' to a focus. In fact, a person suffering from what James calls 'habit neurosis' lives with only one beam switched on; the right-brain has lost interest in life. The result is 'life failure', the feeling that nothing is worth doing.

And here we come to the heart of the matter, the real problem of human existence. It is this power of habit to *rob us of all sense of reality.* In this sense we are all dual-personalities; for half the time we are striving and struggling to stay alive and improve our lot; the other half, we accept the present as if there was no reality beyond it, and lapse into a kind of hypnotic trance. Seen objectively, there is something almost macabre about this duality, a touch of Jekyll and Hyde. It is like meeting a man of impressive personality and powerful intellect who suddenly sucks his thumb and lapses into baby talk.

Let me try to be more specific. I spend my day writing about the peculiarities of the human mind and our ability to slip into the 'other mode' of consciousness. Periodically, as I write, I remember that a boxed set of the Beethoven symphonies conducted by Mengelberg arrived this morning, and each time, I feel a glow of satisfaction; I am looking forward to comparing his version of the Ninth with Fürt-wangler's. At the end of the day, I relax in my armchair, pour myself a glass of wine, and watch the TV news. Now it is time to play the Mengelberg; but somehow, I have lost interest. Is it really worth the effort of finding the Fürtwangler set? I put on a record, but I am not really listening; I am glancing at a book someone has sent me for review. . . . And tomorrow, I shall wonder why I didn't stick to my original intention of comparing Mengelberg and Fürtwangler, for now the idea strikes me again as fascinating. . . .

What happened? Well, quite simply: at a crucial point, my 'robot' took over. My relaxation triggered an automatic response, almost like the post-hypnotic suggestion that can cause a person to fall asleep when a certain key word is repeated. I relaxed – and then, in effect, I over-relaxed and fell asleep.

To blame the 'robot' would be absurd; he is only a convenience, like the housewife's washing machine. The trouble lies in ourselves: in this curious failure of the sense of reality. This deficient sense of reality seems to lie, for example, at the root of all mental illness. Consider what happens when someone begins to feel 'run down'. Life begins to seem repetitive and futile; it costs an effort to get through the working day. Then he takes a fishing holiday, and within a couple of weeks is feeling cheerful and alive and ready to face the winter. What precisely has happened? Well, it sounds absurd when expressed in so many words: but what has happened is that the holiday has convinced him of the real existence of the rest of the world. As he sits watching his float bobbing on the water, something inside him gives a sigh of *relief*, as if he has just received some news that took a weight off his mind. And if he tried to express his feeling in words, he would say: 'My God, I'd forgotten that this place existed.' If you said: 'Are you trying to tell me that you literally forgot that there was such a place as Scotland?', he would answer: 'Not quite. But I'd somehow stopped believing in it.' And we can all perfectly well understand this paradoxical statement (which would certainly baffle a Martian): that you can somehow *know* a place exists, and yet not believe it.

The explanation lies in the simple fact that before we can 'know' something, it has to *sink in*. A child is born into a narrow little world of its cradle and its mother's arms; it knows nothing of the 'outside world'. Gradually, the area of its experience is extended – to other rooms, to the garden, to the street outside, to the park. Each step gives it a wider range of experience, and it envies its elder brothers and sisters who go to school, and seem to lead far more 'grown up' lives. The craving for a wider range of experience is fundamental to all of us. But then, there is another kind of experience, which is at once more exciting and less real than the street and the park: the experience that comes through television and books. *This* is where the dichotomy seems to begin. We know the Wild West exists, but we don't really believe it. In order to really believe it, we would need to have been there.

Which brings us back to that mysterious paradox. For the man on the fishing holiday *has* been there before. Yet he has still somehow 'forgotten' it.

And *what* has he forgotten? Not just the existence of that particular place. What he experiences as he steps outdoors with his fishing rod, and recognises that smell of evaporating dew, is far more complex. It awakens echoes inside him, memories of other times and places, a sense of the sheer bigness of the world, of its multiplicity and excitement.

But these, in turn, are what drive us to effort. When a man achieves something he has wanted for a long time, he feels an enormous sense of satisfaction at the thought that *he has not allowed himself to be discouraged*, not allowed himself to lapse into mistrust and life-devaluation. At the same time, he glimpses the real menace of forgetfulness: that it causes us to spend our lives half-asleep, that it turns us into inefficient machines who never realise a quarter of our potentialities. It is not the drive and will-power that we lack. Show us a goal that touches deep springs of excitement, and nothing can stop us. Our real trouble lies in that deficient sense of reality, our tendency to forget the goal even after we have seen it.

Suddenly, it is possible to see what has gone wrong with human evolution. Animals have no sense of purpose beyond their instincts – for self-preservation, for reproduction, for territory. They are trapped in the present. Man has developed conceptual consciousness, the power to grasp a far wider range of experience, to remember distant goals. This *far-sightedness* is so far beyond that of any other animal that, in theory, we ought to be little short of god-like.

Then what has gone wrong? Quite simply: that although we possess this power – which has been bequeathed to us from thousands of generations of evolution – we make so little use of it that we might as well be cows grazing in a field. Like the animals, we also spend most of our time stuck in the present. We bumble along short-sightedly, obsessed by the needs of the moment, deriving no real advantage from the power that distinguishes us from whales and chimpanzees. It is as absurd as owning an expensive Rolls-Royce and keeping it permanently in the garage. We have forgotten why we bought it: that it can transport us to new scenes and distant places, that it can open our minds to new possibilities. In effect, we have started to travel along a completely new path of evolution, then forgotten why we set out. Instead of marching, we are sitting by the roadside, trying to think up ways of passing the time.

And how has this strange situation come about? Through a *polarisation* of our powers. Psychologically speaking, we consist of three major components: the left-brain, the right-brain, and the 'robot' (probably located in the cerebellum). The purpose of the left-brain is to 'cope', to deal with immediacy. The purpose of the right-brain is to make us aware of meanings, of over-all patterns. The purpose of the robot is to mechanise our learning, so we can get on and learn something else. What has happened is that the left-brain and the robot have formed an alliance, a kind of business-partnership, aimed at guaranteeing our survival. It has been fantastically successful, but there is one drawback: it has robbed us of all sense of *urgency*. It tells us that tomorrow will be more-or-less like today and yesterday, and that conse-

quently, our only aim is to keep out of trouble and stay alive.
And since the right-brain was always the silent partner, it can
do very little about it except mutter under its breath and
dream about the coming revolution that will break up this
dreary alliance. (In fact, as we shall see in a later chapter, the
right-brain and the robot have their own alliance, whose
consequences are just as disastrous.)

Consider the way the alliance operates. The left is coping
with its everyday tasks with the aid of the robot; it does this
efficiently, but without much enthusiasm, for it 'takes them
for granted'. Suddenly, an emergency arises. The left
instantly dismisses the robot; it cannot afford to make any
mistakes. It demands an assessment of the problem, and the
right obligingly provides this, together with a flood of surplus
energy.

Suddenly, the left is no longer bored. It is gripped by a
sense of purpose. It can see that failure could lead to a
chain-reaction of failures and defeats. With a powerful sense
of urgency, it proceeds to take decisions and give orders.

But with this kind of teamwork, the problem already
begins to look less serious. The left begins to lose its sense of
urgency, and hands over some of its tasks to the robot again.
The right ceases to provide surplus energy, and again begins
to feel 'left out'. And the left wonders why it is again feeling
bored and tired.

This, then, explains why human beings fail to take
advantage of their 'far-sightedness', and why they seem to
have got 'stuck' at this point in their evolution. The three
components are so arranged that they actively interfere with
one another – rather like a car in which the brake, accelerator
and clutch are placed so close together that you cannot brake
without accelerating or depressing the clutch. . . .

What *should* happen can be seen whenever we experience
those brief moods of 'reality' – 'holiday consciousness' – in
which everything becomes sharp and clear, like Wordsworth's
view of London, 'all bright and glittering in the smokeless
air'. What strikes us with a kind of amazement in such
moments is the 'interestingness' of the world, its endlessly

fascinating complexity. This is right-brain perception, *meaning* perception.

And what is perfectly obvious in such moments is that if only we could maintain this level of meaning-perception, all our problems would disappear. It fills us with excitement and courage, and the sense of endless vistas of possibility induces a kind of incredulity that human beings could ever suffer from boredom. In Dürrenmatt's play *An Angel Comes to Babylon*, one of the characters asks the angel why human life is so full of suffering. The angel regards her with astonishment and says: 'My dear young lady, I have travelled the world from end to end, and I can assure you that there is not the slightest sign of suffering.' And the moments of 'holiday consciousness' bring that same absurd perception: that most suffering is really the result of 'habit neurosis'. Human beings are a hundred times stronger than they ever realise. As James says: 'We live subject to arrest by degrees of fatigue which we have come only from habit to obey.' As Graham Greene's 'whiskey priest' in *The Power and the Glory* stands in front of a firing squad, he has the sudden perception that 'it would have been so easy to be a saint'. The threat of death has *awakened* him to the realisation that what he regarded as insurmountable barriers are really as surmountable as a five-barred gate.

No animal is capable of such a vision, because no animal possesses our 'conceptual consciousness', this power to see into the distance. What it means, then, is that human beings possess a possibility that is open to no other creature on earth: of *breaking through* to a new evolutionary level of vision and purpose. All that is necessary is for us to solve this simple mechanical problem: how, so to speak, to rearrange the brake, accelerator and clutch until they stop interfering with one another. Solve that, and we shall have learned the secret of how to turn men into creatures like Dürrenmatt's angel.

There are several approaches to this problem, and they deserve a chapter to themselves.

# FOUR

# Frankenstein's Castle

IN THE MID 1950s, a book called *A Drug Taker's Notes* was published in England; it described the writer's experiences with the 'psychedelic' drug lysergic acid. The author, R. H. Ward, was a great deal less well-known than Aldous Huxley, whose own account of his 'psychedelic' experiences, *The Doors of Perception*, had created a sensation in 1953. Ward's book aroused far less interest; which is a pity, for it is, in its way, as important as Huxley's.

The opening chapter contains an account of an early experience with nitrous oxide, used as a dental anaesthetic. He says: 'On this occasion, it seemed to me that I passed, after the first few inhalations of the gas, directly into a state of consciousness already far more complete than the fullest degree of ordinary waking consciousness, and that I then passed progressively upwards (for there was an actual sensation of upward movement) into finer and finer degrees of heightened awareness.' He records his surprise that he was still able to think, and was not being made unconscious by the gas. He speaks of 'an extraordinary sense of the *rightness of things*', and says: 'While it was altogether strange, this new condition was also familiar; it was even in some sense my rightful condition.'

Perhaps the most important phrase here is 'a state of consciousness already far more complete than the fullest degree of ordinary waking consciousness'. This is the most difficult thing for us to grasp: that everyday consciousness is not a kind of absolute, a state that 'tells us the truth' about the world. It *is* a 'mirror of reality' – but only a very small and tarnished pocket mirror.

After taking the psychedelic drug, Ward observed what

Aldous Huxley had also described: the disappearance of the sense of time. And since we know that the right-brain, unlike the left, has no sense of time, then it is a reasonable assumption that one of the effects of the drug is to put the left-brain out of action. In fact, the precise effect is still not understood; all that is known for certain is that it seems to work by blocking the activity of a nerve hormone called serotonin. And this in itself is an exciting discovery; for serotonin seems to be a substance with unusual properties. There seems to be a definite connection between serotonin and evolution: at least, the primates have more serotonin in their bodies than any other creature. One of its functions is to inhibit sexual development. And since intellectuality and early sexual development seldom seem to go together, serotonin is probably linked with intellectual development. (It may or may not be coincidence, but the figs of the tree known as *ficus religiosus*, or bó-tree, under which the Buddha achieved enlightenment, have an exceptionally high serotonin content.)

Only a very tiny proportion of the body's serotonin is to be found in the brain (in the body it acts as a neuro-transmitter); but that tiny percentage seems to be of immense importance. Schizophrenic patients have far less serotonin in the brain than normal people. And since it is believed that the brain's serotonin channels nerve messages in an orderly manner, we may again surmise that serotonin is somehow connected with clear thinking and with 'insight'.

Serotonin is also connected with that mysterious part of the brain called the pineal gland, or 'pineal eye'. The Hindu religious tradition asserts that the pineal eye – or 'third eye' – is man's 'spiritual centre'. In the occult tradition, the pineal gland is responsible for extra-sensory perception; the researches of Sir Alexander Cannon revealed that mediums have larger pineal glands than most people.

It seems strange that the ancient Hindus and Tibetans probably knew about the pineal gland, since it is an extremely tiny organ that weighs less than a tenth of a gram. It has another peculiarity. Our brains – as I have remarked earlier – are divided into two identical halves, as if a mirror had been placed down the middle; only the pineal gland has no 'double'. The Hindus also seem to have been correct in calling it an eye. In the *Tuatara* lizard of New Zealand it can be clearly recognised as an eye, under a transparent membrane in the top of the skull, complete with pigmented retina and lens. Yet even in this lizard, it has become a 'vestigial organ', like the appendix. In men and animals, the pineal eye has gradually become 'buried' in the depth of the brain, until it is now to be found in the mid-brain, between the cerebellum and the thalamus.

It has been recognised as a gland for many centuries; Descartes thought it was the point in man where body and soul are joined together. The novelist Smollett makes his 'atom' (in *Adventures of an Atom*) declare that it can only communicate with men once it is inside their pineal gland. But it was not until 1958 that the pineal eye was proved to be a gland; Aaron B. Lerner of Yale isolated its hormone, melatonin. This, again, seems to be a curious substance. Melatonin means 'darkness constricting'; injected into various creatures, it turns them a lighter colour. Melatonin seems to be involved in our circadian biorhythms. But it also seems to have a definite 'preference' for darkness. When rats are kept in non-stop light, their pineal glands grow smaller, and they show premature sexual development. And – most significant – melatonin is manufactured by the pineal gland from serotonin. (It is tempting to speculate that the poet's love of the night and darkness may be due to this preference of his pineal gland for the element that permits it to develop. . . .)

It begins to look, then, as if serotonin and melatonin are somehow connected to man's 'higher functions' – as the Hindu tradition suggests. Yet drugs like mescalin and lysergic acid produce their effect by *blocking* the action of serotonin. Again, not enough is known about these matters; but one theory could be summarised as follows. The brain is a kind of Frankenstein's Castle, and serotonin is the jailer, who goes around with the keys at his belt, able to unlock hidden rooms and release their 'unconscious' occupants. He does this in a careful and orderly manner, and we must suppose that he is one of the most important servants of the left cerebral hemisphere. Drugs like mescalin and LSD paralyse the jailer, and proceed to open doors with their own skeleton keys. They stroll into the right-brain and release its long-inhibited powers. This is why Ward and Huxley experienced a heightening of reality: the right's job is to communicate *meaning*.

But we must also bear in mind that the right-brain has something of a criminal record – as we can see in Louis Vivé, May Naylor, Sally Beauchamp, Esther Cox. Psychedelic drugs can let 'Russian man' out of his prison. And, since this Frankenstein's Castle is full of secret rooms, there is no telling what other monsters are waiting their chance to stagger into the daylight. . . .

We are not sure what role the pineal gland plays in this peculiar drama; but it is certainly important. In *The Parable of the Beast*, John Bleibtreu remarks that the word ecstasy means to 'stand outside', and also to derange, then goes on to say: 'It is becoming more and more difficult to avoid concluding that if ecstasy has any material biochemical basis in being, the biochemical substances controlling both its sexual and transcendental manifestations are probably manufactured in the pineal gland.' But then, ecstasy is frequently connected with insight, with flashes of 'enlightenment'. In insight, we 'stand outside' our usual involvement in our emotional and physical processes, and seem to experience a glimpse of a purely objective consciousness. It seems, then, just conceivable that the pineal gland could be the mediator between the two hemispheres, and the key to human evolution.

Now Huxley was so excited by the power of mescalin to 'amplify' his sense of meaning that he suggested that it ought to be as available as alcohol or tobacco. Even so, he admitted that it had one interesting drawback. 'The mind was primarily concerned, not with measures and locations, but with being and meaning. And along with indifference to space there went an even completer indifference to time. "There seems to be plenty of it", was all I would answer when the investigator asked me what I felt about time.' This is, of course, what one would expect from someone immersed in right-brain consciousness. But our sense of space and time is vital to our survival. Huxley points out that the nervous system is really a kind of 'reducing valve' to prevent us from being overwhelmed by too much meaning. 'What comes out at the other end is a measly trickle of the kind of consciousness which will help us to stay alive on the surface of this particular planet.'

In which case, too much indulgence in psychedelic drugs could conceivably be dangerous. One of my friends who took mescalin – the novelist Laura del Rivo – said that the piles of dirty dishes in the kitchen looked so beautiful that washing-up seemed irrelevant. If psychedelic drugs were unlimitedly available, the result would probably be a repetition of the history of nineteenth-century romanticism, but on a larger scale: that is, a sharp increase in the number of dreamers who find real life dreary and intolerable.

The other major drawback is touched upon by R. H. Ward: the bad trip, the possibility of releasing some misshapen Quasimodo from one of the locked rooms. When Sartre took mescalin in 1936 in Saint-Anne's hospital, he was immediately plunged into a nightmare world in which he was attacked by an octopus, followed around by a giant lobster, and spied on by an orang-utan. Sartre's basic outlook on life was clearly one of mistrust and hostility; with his left-brain censor reduced to impotence, he was at the mercy of juvenile delinquent who lives in the right. For months after his mescalin trip, Sartre believed he was going insane.

My own experience of mescalin is described in the appendix of *Beyond the Outsider*. My 'trip' was pleasant enough, although I experienced none of the visual effects described by Huxley; I was plunged into an agreeable but sluggish dreaminess. In this torpid state, I became aware of the problem mentioned by Huxley: 'How was this cleansed perception to be reconciled with a proper concern with human relations . . . ?' – in my case, with my concern for my wife and three-year-old daughter? Although I personally felt nothing but a sense of relaxation and trustfulness, I was aware that, in practice, the world is full of dangers, and that in this state, I was incapable of the necessary vigilance; it made me feel guilty. I was neglecting my job of looking after them. Moreover, my ability to think was impaired. Huxley remarks that he found his own ability to remember and 'think straight' little, if at all, reduced. I could 'think straight', but I could not think to any purpose. Even the feeling of universal love was not particularly pleasant; I compared it to having a large alsatian dog who puts his paws on your shoulders and licks your face.

My experience made me clearly aware of the real objection to psychedelic drugs: their effects are not controllable. Ideally, we should be able to *move freely* between left- and right-brain consciousness. Too much left-brain consciousness may be bad for us, but to put it out of action with mescalin is like swatting a fly with a sledgehammer. Less violent methods are required.

In a novel called *A Room in Cairo*, the French writer Albert Cossery argues persuasively that marihuana-smoking is such a method. His hero, Gohar, is a gentle, courteous being who possesses nothing, and sleeps on a dirty mattress on the floor. Everybody is fond of him, for hashish enables him to maintain a kindly, detached view of human existence. At one point in the novel, deprived of his hashish, he strangles a prostitute. But this, the author implies, is simply an unpleasant accident, the last thing in the world that his hero would do a second time. Gohar is a peaceable man, a philosopher who has withdrawn from the rat-race – which, like Omar Khayyám, he contemplates with kindly superiority. If more people were like him, the world would be a better place. . . .

In fact, Gohar uses hashish to live a right-brain existence, to save him from the tyranny of the left. *A Room In Cairo* is an argument in favour of right-brain consciousness. And there can be no doubt that hashish *is* preferable to mescalin or LSD as a method of achieving right-brain awareness – its effects are so much less drastic. But the basic objection is the same. If all men spent their time drifting serenely in a state of right-brain consciousness, civilisation would collapse. Left-brain awareness, with all its corollaries of alienation and neurosis, is the essential prelude to the building of civilisation.

In fact, it is arguable that man *was* once essentially a right-brain creature. The suggestion has received its latest and most brilliant exposition in *The Origin of Consciousness in the Break-down of the Bicameral Mind* by Dr Julian Jaynes of Princeton. Jaynes has argued that as recently as five thousand years ago, the human brain had no kind of ego-awareness. Man was a kind of slot-machine, reacting spontaneously to external stimuli without ever asking himself: 'What shall I do now?' – for the simple reason that he had no sense of 'I'. Jaynes believes that when he had to make decisions, he heard 'voices', which emanated from the right side of his brain, and which he took to be the voices of the gods. It was only through the development of writing, and through various catastrophes that demanded a new level of self-awareness, that man achieved the ability to look *in* on himself as well as out towards the world.

This second part of the theory – the development of an independent, left-brain ego – is self-evidently true. The notion that ancient man had a divided brain is altogether more questionable. When we relax into 'intuitive consciousness', the reverse seems to happen – the walls between the ego and that 'other self' seem to dissolve, plunging us into a kind of twilight world of feeling which is probably close to the kind of consciousness experienced by cows. This suggests that, far from having a divided (or 'bicameral') mind, ancient man's brain was uni-cameral. As writing developed and catastrophes overwhelmed him (the chief of these seems to have been the invasion of the Mediterranean by the 'Sea Peoples' around 1200 BC), he had to drag himself out of this uni-cameral consciousness, and create a more precise and powerful left-brain awareness. Jaynes's major contribution is to muster so much archaeological evidence to demonstrate the gradual emergence of the new ego-consciousness after about 2500 BC.

This, then, is why drugs like mescalin and hashish are no solution to the problem of creating a new level of co-operation between left and right. Man has already been that way.

What this means, in effect, is that we must reject all theories that tell us that civilisation was basically a mistake. Jean-Jacques Rousseau was the first to base a whole philosophy upon this alluring piece of wishful-thinking, and to suggest that man would do better to go 'back to nature'. Nearly two centuries later, Freud elaborated the same idea in *Civilisation and Its Discontents*, arguing that civilised man is bound to be unhappy because civilisation is based on the repression of his natural impulses – particularly the sexual impulse. Civilisation *means* frustration.

It was a contemporary of Rousseau, Donatien-Alphonse-François de Sade, who carried these views to their logical extreme and – unintentionally – demonstrated their absurdity. According to Sade, if man wishes to realise his potentialities and be truly 'free', he must reject civilisation and its artificial laws – particularly its religion and morality. The natural appetites must be allowed to express themselves freely and openly, without shame. So the heroine of an early story, Eugénie de Franval, is brought up by her father without any knowledge of morality or religion; as a consequence she is simple, pure and open hearted. And when her father makes sexual advances, she surrenders without any qualms and thoroughly enjoys it. And in *Philosophy in the Bedroom*, another Eugénie is introduced to sex by a debauched brother and sister, and finds it so delightful that she agrees that all 'moral' prohibitions should be scornfully ignored. They tell her: 'In whatever circumstances, a woman . . . should have no other aim than to be fucked from morning to night. . . .'

But Sade is not intelligent enough to see that natural, straightforward sex from morning to night would bore the most enthusiastic nymphomaniac. What Sade finds so exciting is not 'natural' sex, but sex artificially heightened by the feeling that he is being wicked – in other words, by the very civilised standards he thinks he is ignoring. In the later novels, this becomes self-evident as his heroes indulge in murder, torture and every form of sex crime. The harder he tries to prove that man would be free without his inhibitions, the more he demonstrates that he cannot be free without inhibitions to react *against*. Sade's conception of freedom is totally negative. What would he do if he found himself in a society in which all his pet hatreds had disappeared – the Church, the aristocracy, the law?

He would sink into a kind of inner-vacuum, a state of blank, unmitigated boredom and emptiness.

The only thing Sade succeeded in 'proving' is that freedom cannot be purchased by the rejection of civilisation. For better or worse, man has developed this obsessive, left-brain ego with its passion for order. There is no going back.

But how do we go forward?

One thing that is clear is that we need to learn how to avoid being *trapped* in left-brain consciousness. Everybody knows how this comes about; we push ourselves too hard. Perhaps I have to drive someone to the station, and I realise I have not left myself enough time. Every traffic light is against me; every time I turn a corner I encounter a traffic jam. By the time I arrive, I am 'locked' in a state of hypertension. And it is practically impossible to 'unwind', because once I am in this state, almost anything can make me 'tighten up' again. If I remain in this state too long, I begin to experience what I call 'the burning rubber smell', a feeling like trying to drive with the brakes on.

In the 1930s, a young Viennese doctor named Hans Selye became aware that many physical illnesses are caused by psychological 'stress'. The body possesses a 'homeostatic system' – the ability to *adjust itself* to strains and illnesses, and keep itself, so to speak, on an even keel. Stress can weaken this power to adjust, so the patient succumbs to an illness he would normally throw off.

We have already noted – in an earlier chapter – how the French physician Charcot discovered that hysterical patients could be cured by hypnosis. A Frenchman, Emile Coué, and a German, Johannes Schult, followed up this discovery by recognising that a hypnotised patient is cured by his *own* will rather than that of the hypnotist. It was 'auto-suggestion'. Coué used to make his patients repeat: 'Every day in every way I am becoming better and better', and although the formula aroused derision among his medical colleagues, it worked. In a small French village, a doctor named Auguste Liébault found that he could cure all kinds of illnesses by soothing the patient into a hypnotic sleep and telling them that they would wake up cured. In 1882, he tried the same method on a patient of the famous neurologist Hyppolyte Bernheim, and cured him of a sciatica that had defied Bernheim's efforts. Bernheim was so impressed that he also began to employ hypnosis. But he also came to the conclusion that the patient really cures himself, and that therefore suggestion works just as well on a wide-awake patient. It worked so well that Bernheim gradually came to abandon hypnosis.

We can see that what really happens is that the left brain weakens the homeostatic system through over-anxiety, producing illness. Auto-suggestion persuades the right-brain to exert its powers, and repairs the homeostatic system.

In the late 1950s Dr Joe Kamiya of the Langley-Porter Neuropsychiatric Institute in San Francisco noted that when people experience a state of serenity and relaxation, an EEG machine (electro-encephalograph, for measuring brain-waves) shows that the brain is producing alpha rhythms, waves with a frequency of eight to twelve cycles per second. The moment the person experiences tension, the rhythms switch to beta, a faster rhythm at fourteen or so cycles per second. He also discovered that if the EEG machine gave a soft bleeping noise when the rhythms went into alpha, the subject could quickly learn to turn the alpha state on and off at will. If he chose to maintain the alpha state, he could sink into moods of deep serenity or contemplation. To actually be able to *see* the alpha rhythms on a screen, or hear them as a sound, allowed the subject to develop the trick of controlling them. Abraham Maslow was immensely excited by this discovery, recognising that Kamiya had, in effect, stumbled upon a method for inducing the peak experience.

Bio-feedback – as the technique came to be called – can indeed induce states of 'controlled serenity', apparently identical with the states of deep meditation that are the aim of such disciplines as yoga and zazen – the latter is Japanese for 'sitting in meditation'. When EEG machines were fitted to Zen adepts and 'transcendental meditators' – followers of the Maharishi Mahesh Yogi – they revealed that they were also able to maintain alpha states at will, oblivious of external stimuli (such as the ringing of a bell). Dr Robert Wallace of the Center for the Health Sciences in Los Angeles, also discovered that transcendental meditators could reduce their oxygen intake by a fifth in a matter of minutes (it takes the rest of us a good night's sleep), slow down the heartbeat, and achieve a 'fourth state of consciousness' distinct from wakefulness, dreamless sleep, and dreaming: a sustained 'trance'. Dr Barbara Brown of the Sepulveda Veterans Administration Hospital in Southern California has elaborated bio-feedback techniques – using colours on a screen – until her subjects can control heartbeat, muscle activity, stomach activity, even body temperature, by studying this visual code.

As if these discoveries were not startling enough, a behavioural psychologist, Dr Neal Miller of Rockefeller University, demonstrated that his laboratory rats could be 'trained' (by the Pavlovian reward system) to control their heartbeats, blood pressure and rate of salivation. This had been considered an obvious impossibility by his colleagues because such functions as heartbeat and digestion are controlled by our 'autonomic nervous system', which is not supposed to be within our conscious control. Hypnotists, of course, have always known that they can control – or cause the patient to control – the autonomic nervous system: they can even cause warts to disappear. But Miller's experiments revealed that such control is not a freak-ability possessed by human beings; it seems to extend throughout the animal kingdom.

But in view of what we know about the 'two people' living inside our heads, this result becomes less surprising. We may say, as a kind of preliminary working hypothesis, that the left looks outward, the right inward. The left 'copes' with the external world; the right controls our inner-world (no doubt through the mediation of other parts of the brain). So control of our 'automatic' functions is simply a matter of persuading that 'other self' to issue the orders. And the right is perfectly willing to do this if it receives a request of sufficient authority, either from some external source (including the hypnotist) or from the left-brain ego.

We can also see that beta rhythms – associated with action

and problem-solving – seem to be the characteristic 'voice' of the left, while the relaxed alpha rhythms characterise the right. (This is not, of course, to say that either side has a monopoly of one or the other.) Bio-feedback could therefore be regarded as a technique for shifting the 'personal centre of gravity' from the left towards the right.

Bio-feedback is obviously a discovery of major import-ance. But is it the solution to the problem of the 'other mode' of consciousness? Undoubtedly, it comes closer to the solution than LSD or marihuana because it *is* a method based on conscious control. A person who can induce 'alpha con-sciousness' at will can never become a slave of the 'false self'. His resistance to mental strains and tensions – the 'smell of burning rubber' – should be far greater than that of non-relaxors. A society in which bio-feedback techniques were taught at school would undoubtedly be closer to Utopia than anything the world has seen so far. But, in the last analysis, it is open to the same objection that William James raised against the Chautauqua Community – that after a week of 'charm and ease' he found himself heaving a sigh of relief and saying 'Ouf! . . . now for something primordial and savage . . .'. For better or worse, human life is a struggle. Man is fundamentally a problem-solver. As Nietzsche says, we are at our best when overcoming obstacles, breaking down barriers.

To put it another way: the alpha-state is a *passive* type of 'peak experience'. It is important to distinguish between passive and active. The kind of deep serenity Wordsworth experienced on Westminster Bridge is the passive peak experience; the intensity described by Yeats:

> When a man is fighting mad,
> Something drops from eyes long blind,
> He completes his partial mind. . . .

is the active peak experience. The alpha-state can certainly be the springboard to the active peak experience; but it is not necessarily so.

That is to say: alpha-states are an important step towards

the control of consciousness; but they are no more than a step.

The point may be underlined by a story told of Aleister Crowley by the American writer William Seabrook. In 1920 a film actress named Jane Wolfe arrived at Crowley's 'abbey' on Cefalu, hoping that Crowley could cure her of her various problems, including depression and the results of too much bootleg gin. Crowley suggested that she should take up a 'magical retirement' on an isolated promontory overlooking the sea; it would be necessary, he told her, to stay there for a month. The idea horrified her, but Crowley insisted. Her shelter was a tent and a nearby cave. She was to wear only a woollen robe. Her food would consist of a loaf of bread, a bunch of grapes and a jug of water every day.

During the first days of her vigil she was bored, resentful, miserable and uncomfortable. A week later she was merely paralysed with boredom. Then, in the last ten days or so, she suddenly experienced an immense, deep sense of calm, 'deep joy, renewal of strength and courage'. Crowley had recognised that her problem was the 'false self' created by the New York 'rat race'. She had become so dominated by hypertension that she had forgotten how to relax. The 'false self' had to be persuaded that it could safely go off-duty. When this finally happened, she relaxed into the alpha-state, right-brain consciousness.

It is clear that Crowley understood about the 'false self' and right-brain awareness, and could induce these states in himself. But while Crowley's 'powers' were undoubtedly remarkable, all accounts of his personality make it clear that they were not matched by his qualities as a human being; he could be spoilt, selfish, resentful and downright sadistic. And his autobiography, the *Confessions*, reveals him as a curiously limited person; he had advanced just so far, then reached some kind of limit. Whatever control of alpha states he had achieved (and as a yogi he seems to have reached an advanced level), he remained trapped in personality, the left-brain ego.

The question, it seems, is not simply one of inducing alpha-states, and achieving freedom from the absurd hypertensions of the left. It is of *how far* the personal centre of gravity can be moved towards the 'right'. Genuine mystical experience seems to involve a different kind of insight, in which the mystic somehow *loses touch* with his 'normal personality'. This can be illustrated in the experience of the Silesian mystic Jacob Boehme. Bishop Martensen describes how 'sitting one day in his room, his eye fell upon a burnished pewter dish, which reflected the sunshine with such marvellous splendour that he fell into an inward ecstasy, and it seemed to him as if he could now look into the principles and deepest foundations of things. He believed that it was only a fancy, and in order to banish it from his mind he went out into the green fields. But here he noticed he could gaze into the very heart of things, the very herbs and grass, and that actual nature harmonised with what he had inwardly seen. . . .' And Boehme himself wrote: 'In one quarter of an hour I saw and knew more than if I had been many years together at a university.' But he adds that although he was able to understand all things, 'I could very hardly apprehend the same in my external man.' His 'external man' is the everyday personality, with its logical categories. Boehme's vision had separated him from this everyday self, swept him so far towards 'the right' that he lost touch with his personal landmarks.

Again, the phrase about knowing more 'than if I had been many years together at a university' expresses another basic characteristic of the mystical experience – the sense of 'bird's-eye vision', some over-all view of reality, a vast *pattern*. This seems to confirm that we are dealing with 'right-brain awareness', since the business of the right-hemisphere is pattern recognition. William James once described a flash of mystical awareness in which, he says, some memory reminded him of something else, and this reminded him of something else, until, like a flash of lightning zig-zagging out to the horizon, he was overwhelmed by a 'sudden vision of ranges of distant facts of which I could give no articulate account.' And in an autobiographical story called *The Abominable Mr Gunn*, Robert Graves has described how, as a schoolboy, he had a similar vision while sitting on the roller behind the cricket pavilion, as a result of which he 'knew everything'. The insight remained with him for the next twelve hours or so, and only disappeared for good when he tried to write it down.

What seems to happen in such cases is that the right-brain provides some immense, over-all sense of pattern. Graves says: 'To be plain: though conscious of having come less than a third of the way along the path of formal education . . . I nevertheless held the key of truth in my hand, and could use it to open the lock of any door. Mine was no religious or philosophical theory but a simple method of looking sideways at disorderly facts to make perfect sense of them.'

'Sideways' is perhaps the wrong word. What he seems to mean, rather, is the way that we can look at something 'out of the corner of the eye' and instantly grasp its significance. In other words, the 'pattern-creating' faculty of the right-brain is at work. But it operates so swiftly – in fact, instantaneously – that the left-brain is unable to analyse the pattern. Bertrand Russell says: 'The sense of certainty and revelation comes before any definite belief' – that is, what is seen comes before what is known. Volume after volume about mysticism underlines the same point. Plotinus says (in the fifth Ennead) that the 'vision' needs no special gift or effort, but only *the use of a faculty which all possess but few employ*. That is to say, this 'other mode' of consciousness is not in any way remote from everyday consciousness; it lies right at the side of it, only a fraction of a millimetre away. It is seen, like a lightning flash, in all moments of joy and relief, as our *deliberately limited* left-brain perception is replaced by a wider pattern.

In one of the most important books about mysticism, *The Timeless Moment*, Warner Allen says that the real problem is that consciousness has a dual nature; ego is not only aware of itself, but also of non-ego. This, says Allen, is the apparently insoluble paradox of mysticism. His book was published in 1946. Twenty years later, Sperry's discovery of the two 'selves' inhabiting the brain had solved the insoluble.

# FIVE

# The Powers of the Right

THOMSON J. HUDSON, an American newspaper editor and official of the Patent Office, was in his late fifties when he wrote a book with the unpromising title *The Law of Psychic Phenomena*. It appeared in 1893, and launched Hudson to national and international fame. By 1925, the book had gone through forty-seven printings.

In spite of its title, and in spite of Hudson's frequent references to Jesus in his later writings, *The Law of Psychic Phenomena* is not one of those inspirational volumes about life after death or 'higher spiritual realms'; it is, as its sub-title states, 'A Working Hypothesis for the Systematic Study of the Vast Potential of Man's Mind'. And, what is even more astonishing, it is the first clear statement of the problem of the 'two selves' in modern scientific literature.

He starts from the problem of hypnotic phenomena, as demonstrated by Liébault and Bernheim. Like Freud, he draws the conclusion that man's 'mental organisation' is of a 'dual character'. (Freud, of course, was totally unknown at the time.) 'That is to say, man has, or appears to have, two minds, each endowed with separate and distinct attributes and powers; each capable, under certain conditions, of independent action.' One is the 'objective mind', which deals with the external world through the medium of the five senses. The other is the 'subjective mind', which 'perceives by intuition'. 'It sees without the use of the natural organs of vision,' and is 'that intelligence which makes itself manifest in a hypnotic subject when he is in a state of somnambulism.'

In short, Hudson has recognised the differing functions of the right and left cerebral hemispheres half a century before they were investigated experimentally. It is an incredible piece of intuitive thinking.

Hudson made another basic observation: that the 'objective mind' is capable of reasoning both inductively and deductively, while the subjective mind is only capable of deductive reasoning. Induction is the ability to swoop from a number of given 'facts' to the general principle underlying them: i.e. the recognition of laws. Deductive reasoning starts out from the laws and can predict the facts that follow from them. This seems at first contradictory; surely, if the right-brain ('subjective mind') sees over-all patterns – another name for laws – then it should be capable of reasoning from the particular to the general? The answer is that it can only do so after the left-brain has provided the 'facts'. When the left-brain has provided the trees, the right will recognise a wood. But inductive reasoning is a feedback between left and right. So if the left has been put to sleep by hypnosis, the right can only operate deductively. Its deductions may be as brilliant as those of Sherlock Holmes; but it cannot see its way to new laws or principles. Only the left can do that, with the *aid* of the right.

Again, this makes sense in view of Jaynes's theory of the bicameral mind. At a certain point in his evolution, man began to develop the left-brain ego as an independent unit. Until that time, his discoveries had been merely deductive – fire, the wheel, the plough – all based upon the general principles he recognised in nature. The development of the left-brain ego signalled the rise of science, and the immense and abrupt changes it brought about in the human condition. Man had learned to reason backwards, from the particular to the general. In his primate days, he had swung his body from tree to tree. Now his mind could swing across open spaces. Induction made him into a kind of god.

Much of *The Law of Psychic Phenomena* is concerned with the incredible powers of the 'subjective mind'. He speaks of people who, in a trance-condition, spoke foreign languages they had never learned – although, on investigation, it turned out that they had unconsciously 'absorbed' the languages in childhood, and were simply 'playing them back' like a tape recording. He speaks of artists with 'eidetic' powers – the power to conjure up an image with such total reality that they could sketch it as if it was a solid object present in the room. He tells of a man who was placed in a hypnotic trance and then 'introduced' by the hypnotist to Socrates – and how he then repeated the conversation of the imaginary Socrates, astounding his audience with its brilliance and profundity. One of his most impressive illustrations is a lengthy passage – too long to quote – on the Canadian 'lightning calculator' boy, Zerah Colburn, who, at the age of five, could perform incredible feats of calculation in his head within a matter of seconds. Such questions as the square root of 106,929 were so absurdly simple that he could snap out the answer – 327 – before the questioner had finished speaking. It took him only seconds to say how many minutes there were in forty-eight years – and for good measure, he followed it up by mentioning the number of seconds in the same period. But perhaps his most remarkable feat was his ability to say whether some enormous number is a prime. A prime is a number that cannot be divided by any other whole number – i.e. 5, 7 and 11. Colburn was able to say that 36,083 is a prime. Asked if 4,294,967,297 is a prime, he replied that it could be divided by 641.

But the interesting thing about prime numbers is that there is no general method for discovering whether they can be divided by other numbers – it has to be done by a long process of trial and error. Colburn was doing the *logically impossible*.

Asked how he did the calculations, Colburn always replied that he had no idea – the answer just came into his mind. (In his story *The Abominable Mr Gunn*, Robert Graves describes a schoolfellow named Smilley who had a similar ability, and who was punished by the master until he did his calculations 'normally'.) In other words, Colburn 'saw' the answer – from a bird's-eye view, so to speak. Admirers decided that he ought to receive a mathematical education, so that he would one day be able to explain his 'methods' analytically; in fact, it simply decreased his powers. (We may be reminded that pigeon fanciers used to think that pigeons needed to be trained to find their way back home – until someone tested a young, untrained pigeon, and discovered that it found its way home quicker than the trained ones; the training was only blunting their natural powers.)

The reason that Hudson's book fell out of favour in the 1920s can be found in his chapter on Hypnotism and Mesmerism, in which he states: 'Another prolific source of error which besets the . . . Paris school [Charcot and his followers] consists in its disbelief in . . . the possibility that its subjects may be possessed of clairvoyant or telepathic powers.' For Charcot's scepticism prevailed – so that, for example, in J. Milne Bramwell's standard textbook on hypnotism, published in 1903 (the year Hudson died), a short appendix devoted to clairvoyance and telepathy dismisses them briefly as fraud or self-deception. Yet Charcot's contemporary, Janet himself – emphatically no 'occultist' – commenced his career by studying the case of a woman called Leonie *who could be hypnotised from a distance*. Janet found that he was able to give Leonie a 'mental order' from the other side of Le Havre, and Leonie would 'hear' it telepathically and come and present herself at Janet's house. Janet was able to induce hypnotic trances – at a distance – eighteen times out of twenty-five, and partially in another four. Significantly, Leonie was also a remarkable case of multiple personality, for (as we shall see in a moment) multiple personality often seems to be accompanied by telepathic powers; 'Leonie 1' was a stolid peasant woman, 'Leonie 2' was an excitable, nervous creature, 'Leonie 3' was more intelligent and perceptive than either. (This emergence of a 'superior' personality, far more intelligent than the 'original' self, is one of the most puzzling features of many cases of multiple personality.)

Again, in the 1890s, Professor Paul Joire conducted a series of experiments in telepathy under hypnosis at Lille, and demonstrated clearly that blindfolded subjects could be made to obey purely mental orders. In the 1920s, the Russian L. L. Vasiliev repeated these experiments in Leningrad, and wrote a classic book about them; Vasiliev was also able to place subjects in a hypnotic trance at a distance of thousands of miles, demonstrating that distance appears to be irrelevant to telepathy.

One of the most interesting cases of a scientist forced to acknowledge telepathy is Dr Julian Ochorowitz, of the University of Lemburg. His first paper on psychology appeared when he was 19, in 1869; Ochorowitz was determinedly sceptical about telepathy. In his twenties he became interested in hypnosis, and in 1881 experimented with a 'somnambule' called Mme Lucille. After placing her in a trance, Ochorowitz stood behind her; whenever he moved his hand towards her back, she reacted with muscular tension. Still in trance, she was able to tell him repeatedly which hand was touching her back. When he asked someone else to touch her back, she immediately identified the man. Another subject, a boy, was able to repeat aloud the words Ochorowitz was reading from a book which was held out of sight. One woman 'somnambule' could react to mental suggestions even when her eyes were bandaged and her ears plugged. Yet Ochorowitz remained unconvinced that this was really telepathy – he continued to believe that there must be some natural explanation – for example, that the boy had already read the book he was reading from and was using 'trance memory' to repeat it back, or that the woman was abnormally sensitive to gestures he made behind her back, perhaps able to interpret currents of warm air. When another hypnotic subject achieved a tremendously high score in a card-guessing experiment, Ochorowitz even entertained the hypothesis that he himself had cheated unconsciously.

So when Ochorowitz heard about Janet's experiments with Leonie, he went to Le Havre. He knew Janet was a student of the sceptical Charcot; he was hoping against hope that he and Janet would finally discover the natural explanation of these phenomena. In fact, Leonie finally convinced him of the reality of telepathy. She obeyed complex mental suggestions from a distance – for example, to study a photograph album at eleven the next morning – and reacted violently when the hypnotist made a burn on his wrist in the next room. Awakened from her trance, she still complained that her wrist hurt.

Liébault himself – the man who had started all this – performed similar experiments. While a woman was in a trance, he wrote on a piece of paper that when she woke up, she would see her black hat transformed into a red one; when the woman was awakened, she looked at her hat, and asked who had exchanged it for this red object. . . .

All this allows no conceivable doubt that telepathy-under-hypnosis was demonstrated again and again in the nineteenth century; the most comprehensive book on the subject – Dingwall's *Abnormal Hypnotic Phenomena* – occupies four volumes and covers more than a dozen countries. Yet by the end of the century, it had become an unchallengeable dogma of professional medicine that absolutely no 'abnormal phenomena' occurred under hypnosis. Even the notion that a hypnotised person could call upon unusual strength or endurance was questioned; it was suggested that even an unhypnotised man could, if he tried hard enough, become as stiff as a board, lie between two chairs, and support the weight of a heavy man standing on his stomach.

Equally remarkable are the cases of other forms of 'psychic' abilities demonstrated under hypnosis in the nineteenth century. The Swedish physician Agardh described how a fifteen-year-old boy developed 'clairvoyant' powers after a serious illness. He could read a folded letter with his eyes closed, and describe the title and contents of a book placed against his chest; he was able to tell one woman that she was pregnant – which proved to be true, although she was unaware of it – and another that her ring was of a special kind which concealed an inner-ring. The remarkable French 'somnambule' Alexis Didier repeatedly demonstrated 'travelling clairvoyance' – visiting some distant place under hypnosis, and describing in detail what was happening there. (Again, dozens of such cases are described in the four volumes of *Abnormal Hypnotic Phenomena*.) The hypothesis of telepathy seems to fit many of these cases; yet even here, there are exceptions. A Captain Daniel asked Didier to describe the house of Daniel's father. Didier went into detail about the position of doors, windows, pictures, ornaments and furniture. Daniel said he had made only one mistake – about the colour of the curtains. But when Daniel went to the house after the experiment, he found that Didier had been right after all.

This, then, is why Hudson was able to feel himself on firm ground when he wrote: '[The subjective mind] sees without the use of the natural organs of vision; and . . . it can be made to leave the body, and travel to distant lands and bring back intelligence, oftentimes of the most exact and truthful character. It also has power to read the thoughts of others . . . to read the contents of sealed envelopes and closed books . . .' He devotes a whole chapter of the book to cases of various kinds of 'projection', in which people have succeeded in projecting their thoughts, or their actual physical presence, to distant places.

All this led Hudson to believe that it should be possible to cure sick people at a distance by purely mental means – he called it psycho-therapeutics. He describes trying it on a relative suffering from acute rheumatism and arthritis. The patient was not told, but two other people were taken into his confidence as witnesses. After a few months, one of these two was asked to visit the patient. He found him enormously improved. The improvement had started shortly after Hudson began 'projecting' his healing thoughts.

Understandably, Hudson came to the conclusion that the same basic method was used by Jesus and other healers – the projection of healing influences from the subjective mind. And this probably explains his book's immense popularity – that he appeared to be offering scientific justification for the beliefs of Christianity. In retrospect, this is the least important theory advanced in *The Law of Psychic Phenomena*. The core of the book lies in his recognition that we have two people living inside our heads, and that one of them has almost 'miraculous' powers.

The one psychological oddity that Hudson forgot to mention was the one that might have given him some clue to the mechanisms of 'divided consciousness' – multiple personality. In 1893, the phenomenon was known, but had not yet attracted the widespread attention that came as a result of Morton Prince's book on Sally Beauchamp and Walter Prince's account of the Doris Fischer case. Morton Prince actually has a chapter on 'Sally Beauchamp' as a medium – how one day, as Christine looked in a mirror, her alter-ego Sally began pulling faces at her, and how Christine then succeeded in talking to Sally by asking questions and getting Sally to write her replies on paper. 'Who are you?' 'A spirit.' 'Stuff! Tell the truth . . .' 'Devil, devil, devil. Amen. You'll be sorry when I'm gone. . . .' It might have struck Hudson that the relation between the objective and subjective mind is slightly more complex than he thought. Sally is the subjective mind in revolt. And Hudson might then have found himself considering the poltergeist as another interesting example of the subjective mind in a mischievous mood. Hudson was certain that 'contact with the dead' is an illusion – that the medium is merely picking up dream-messages from the subjective mind. But he failed to draw the inference that the subjective mind actually has – so to speak – a mind of its own.

There is evidence that multiple personalities are more 'psychic' than the rest of us – which is what we might expect. When the objective mind is firmly in control, we suppress our natural 'psychic powers'. Walter Prince tells how, when Doris Fischer was working as a seamstress, she suddenly had an intuitive certainty that her mother was dangerously ill, and rushed home; in fact, her mother was suffering from sudden acute pneumonia, and died later that day. (As a result of the shock, Doris 'split' into yet another personality.) Christine Sizemore, the 'Eve' of *The Three Faces of Eve*, developed certain powers of extra-sensory perception as a by-product of her problems. When she was nine, she took her small sister in the woods, and the child fell in a creek and had to go to bed with a sore throat. In the night, Christine dreamed that Jesus came and told her that her sister had diphtheria. She told her parents, who sent for the doctor; in fact, the child *had* diphtheria. A serum had to be sent for from a hundred miles away, and her life was saved; but for her sister's dream, it would probably have been too late.

She describes other such experiences later in life. She had a premonition that her husband would be electrocuted at work and persuaded him to stay home; the man who took over his job was electrocuted. When her child was about to be vaccinated, she tried to prevent it, saying it would harm her. She was overruled, and the child almost died of a spoiled lot of vaccine. One day she had a premonition that her cousin – hundreds of miles away – was seriously ill, and phoned her home; the cousin was suffering from meningitis. Christine sent her a message saying 'I *will* you to get well' (Hudson's 'healing influence?') and then posted a letter telling her she would be all right. By the time the letter arrived, her cousin had started to recover.

But these experiences can all be explained in terms of telepathy. What is far more puzzling is how the 'subjective mind' can cause poltergeist phenomena: that is, effects that are contrary to the laws of nature. The poltergeist seems to have the mentality of Shakespeare's Puck; its activities are more often mischievous than dangerous. In the classic Stockwell case of January 1772, an elderly lady named Mrs Golding had recently engaged a girl of twenty, Ann Robinson, as a maid. Ten days later the disturbances began: plates hurtled off shelves in the kitchen, a pan of beef shattered, a lock fell to the floor, eggs flew through the air, china and glasses shattered spontaneously, and joints of ham and bacon hanging from the farmhouse ceiling carefully disengaged themselves from their hooks and landed on the floor. A doctor bled Mrs Golding, who was apparently suffering from shock; the blood shot out of the basin, and the basin flew to pieces. When guests were offered a choice between wine or rum, both bottles shattered before they could be uncorked. During the night, tables and chairs flew around with tremendous noise. The racket was so alarming that they were afraid the house might collapse, and the children were sent to the barn, where Ann Robinson helped to dress them; meanwhile, Mrs Golding and other members of the household moved to a house across the way; as soon as Ann Robinson returned, poltergeist effects began there – a coal scuttle turning over, a lantern jumping off its hook to the floor, and candlesticks flying through the air. Back in Mrs Golding's house, a nine-gallon cask of beer was up-ended and a pail of

water 'boiled like a pot'. At this point, Mrs Golding decided
that the maid was responsible, and discharged her on the spot.
As soon as Ann Robinson left, the disturbances ceased.

Here, as in the Rosenheim case mentioned earlier, it seems
probable that Ann Robinson resented having to work, and
her unconscious mind took revenge. She had been in the house
for ten days; we are not told whether, during that time, she had
enjoyed the job; the answer is almost certainly not. It seems
significant that the wine and rum exploded before they could
be uncorked – as if the servant resented these 'gentry' being
offered alcoholic drinks. If the full story were told, it is
probable that we would discover that Ann Robinson found her
employer querulous and despotic, and that by the tenth day she
was in a state of smouldering resentment – a resentment she
was afraid to express openly for fear of losing a good job. Her
'other self', less timid and complaisant, proceeded to express
its opinion of the old lady and her friends.

But *how*? It seems clear that some powerful force can be
utilised by the 'right'; but what is its nature? It seems probable
that it is related to the force used in 'psychokinesis' – when a
'medium' can move small objects by simply staring at them.
Uri Geller's alleged metal bending is also a form of psychokinesis, and Professor John Taylor has suggested that the agent
here may be some electromagnetic force analogous to radio
waves (which, after all, can be used to cook a steak). But there
is no experimental evidence for the existence of such a force.

Another theory has been suggested by the psychical
investigator William Roll, who noted that a number of people
who seemed to cause poltergeist phenomena were epileptics,
and that others showed certain symptoms of epilepsy, like
hallucinations and dissociation. Epilepsy is a discharge of
energy from the central nervous system; and – as we have seen –
the severing of the corpus callosum can cure it. Roll thinks that
this energy could explain the poltergeist.

My own theory is simpler. Good dowsers can go into
convulsions when they stand over water. The force with which
the dowsing rod twists in their hands may break the rod. One
old lady who belongs to the British Society of Dowsers can

dowse with almost anything – one witness described how she picked up an enormous branch as she walked through a wood, and how this swung around in her hand like a huge pointer, indicating the presence of water. Does this force reside in the muscles of the dowser? Or does it flow *through* them from the earth?

The human body certainly seems capable of building energies of a baffling nature. The nature of 'spontaneous combustion' is still a mystery; the only thing that seems fairly certain is that it starts from *inside* the person who is consumed. In his *Letters on Natural Magic*, Sir David Brewster mentions the case of Countess Cornelia Zangari, a lady of sixty-two, who retired to bed in normal health, and was found burned to death the next morning. 'At a distance of four feet from the bed there was a heap of ashes. Her legs, with the stockings on, remained untouched, and the head, half-burned, lay between them. Nearly all the rest of the body was reduced to ashes.' And yet, as in most such cases, the room itself was untouched, except for greasy soot. The blankets of the bed were thrown back as if she had got out of bed in the middle of the night. But apparently she made no outcry – which, again, seems characteristic of spontaneous combustion. There are hundreds of cases on record. In July 1951, a Mrs Reeser of Florida was resting in her armchair when she went up in smoke. All that was left was her skull, shrunken to the size of a baseball, her left foot and a few vertebrae. The armchair lining was burnt; so was a chairside table and the carpet under the chair; otherwise, the apartment was unscathed – except for greasy soot which started four feet above the floor. It was established that a temperature of 3,000 degrees would have been required to incinerate the body to this extent. Michael Harrison's book *Fire From Heaven* documents dozens of similar cases.*

There is probably a connection between spontaneous

---

* Michael Harrison notes that most cases of spontaneous combustion occur near the sea, and speculates that it could be due to the presence of negative ions in the atmosphere.

combustion and cases of 'human electric eels'. In 1877, Caroline Clare, of Bondon, Ontario, suffered from an odd illness that caused her to waste away. Then she began to recover, and turned into a human electric battery. Iron objects would stick to her as if she had turned into an enormous magnet, and people who touched her received severe electric shocks. Jennie Morgan, a fourteen-year-old girl of Sedalia, Missouri, became so highly charged that she could knock a man on his back with a touch of her hand. Louis Hamburger, a sixteen-year-old student of chemistry in Maryland, could pick up a five-pound weight by merely pressing three fingers against it and raising his hand; when he detached his fingers there was a plopping noise, as if suckers were being detached. Frank McKinistry, of Joplin, Missouri, would wake up in the morning with such a powerful electric charge that his feet stuck to the ground, and if he stood still, he was unable to move. A discharge of 'lightning' between his feet would end the current's grip.

In this case, it seems clear that the 'electricity' was not the ordinary force that runs through wires – which would not cause his feet to stick to the ground – but some form of 'static' that had an affinity with earth magnetism. On the other hand, Count John Berenyi of Budapest was able to make a neon tube light up by holding the ends with his hands. The 'force', whatever it is, can behave like a normal electric current.*

In the 1960s the late Robert Ardrey drew widespread attention to the mystery of animal 'homing' in his book *The Territorial Imperative* – a mystery that had been determinedly ignored by science. One theory suggested that salmon found their way back to their home rivers by an incredibly delicate sense of smell. In 1975, a biologist named Richard Blakemore realised that bacteria he was studying under his microscope were being attracted by the earth's magnetic field, and that this explained their mass movements. After this, it was quickly discovered that most – probably all – birds and animals have the same remarkable sensitivity to earth magnetism. In areas

* See *Mysterious Fires and Lights* by Vincent Gaddis.

on the earth's surface where there are magnetic vortices or whirlpools, homing pigeons get hopelessly lost. But the question of which part of the animal is sensitive to the current is still an open one; one suggestion is that some birds have a tiny magnet in the beak. But if, as seems likely, this sensitivity is related to the dowser's ability to react to earth magnetism, then the answer is more likely to be found in the brain.*

In human beings – as we have seen – the dowsing capability seems to lie in the right-brain. If we are correct in assuming that poltergeist activity is also a right-brain phenomenon,† then it seems reasonable to hypothesise a connection between the two – and also between the 'earth forces' and such phenomena as spontaneous combustion and human electric batteries. It seems too great a coincidence that the majority of cases of human electric batteries concern adolescents – just as with poltergeist phenomena. On the other hand, the majority of cases of spontaneous combustion concern elderly persons. Adolescents and elderly persons are both in a state of biological transition; the adolescent is acquiring new powers, while the elderly are in the process of relinquishing theirs. In poltergeist cases and human electric batteries, we get the impression that the power overflows, producing abnormal effects. In the elderly, it seems rather as if the wire can no longer carry the current, and burns out.

But it would probably be a mistake to imagine that we are dealing with purely physical forces – such as earth magnetism, operating through some 'magnetic centre' in the right-cerebral hemisphere. Many poltergeist cases contain examples of the phenomenon known as levitation. Guy Playfair's book, *This House is Haunted*, describing a poltergeist that 'haunted' a house in Enfield in 1977, has photographs of the child concerned floating through the air. But levitation is most commonly associated with religion. There are numerous accounts – and photographs – of Hindu fakirs

---

* A more recent theory suggests it is located under the wings.
† A theory that would still apply even if poltergeist activity involved some form of disembodied spirit.

levitating. Many Christian saints – St Alphonsus Liguori, St Andrew Fournet, St Teresa of Avila, St Joseph of Copertino – were able to levitate. The case of St Joseph of Copertino is the best authenticated. He was a sickly boy who became a Franciscan monk. He was subject to religious ecstasies, and, in the midst of prayers one day, floated over to the altar. From then on, he floated regularly into the air – whenever he was carried away by religious joy – and alighted again as gracefully as a bird. The philosopher Leibnitz and his patron the Duke of Brunswick witnessed the phenomenon, and the Duke was converted to Catholicism. But he was probably mistaken to assume that St Joseph was aided by heavenly powers; this was basically another 'poltergeist effect', brought on by ecstasy, and of no more religious significance than Frank McKinistry's electrical manifestations or Mrs Reeser's spontaneous combustion. What *is* perfectly clear, however, is that Joseph of Copertino's mental state triggered the phenomenon, just as Ann Robinson's state – of suppressed resentment – caused the Stockwell poltergeist effects. Perhaps spontaneous combustion – which usually seems to occur at night – is due to some state of deep depression or mental conflict of the kind that tends to occur if we lie awake at 4 a.m. and brood about trivial problems. . . .

Levitation can also be induced in others. Most people have at some time played the parlour game in which a group of three or four people lift someone by placing only one finger under his knees and armpits. (My own book about Uri Geller contains a photograph of me sailing up into the air as Geller and three others lift me from a chair in this way.) The only preparation that seems to be necessary here is for the 'lifters' to place their hands – on top of one another – on the subject's head, and to press down gently, before disengaging them and lifting. It is possible, of course, that there is a simple physical explanation here – that a spontaneous effort by four people – even using only one finger – exerts far more physical force than might be expected. But a recent letter from a New Zealand correspondent, Sir Jack Harris, describes how he was lifted by a Polish violinist:

'He lifted me with the palm of his hand, the palm being held horizontal . . . so that only one finger of each hand touched me. He was quite a small man and I weigh 15 stone. He repeated this performance on several occasions. It was an eerie sensation – I seemed to rise without any effort. I asked him how he was able to perform this feat, and he explained that he did it by means of suggestion, using my own strength to lift me, and that it was quite easy if you knew how.'

I asked Sir Jack to elaborate and received the following reply:

'As regards my Polish friend, I cannot remember his name, neither can my brother. He was a violinist and a friend of Watkins the publishers. He must be long dead.

'He explained to me that he raised me through the unconscious use of my own strength and life force – in other words, I really lifted myself into the air without realising that I was doing so. He did not think there was anything super-natural about it, merely a matter of learning how to do it.'

'By means of suggestion . . .' Here, again, we are plainly dealing with Hudson's 'subjective mind' and its remarkable powers. But there seems to have been no verbal suggestion. Did the violinist mean that his own assumption that he could lift a 15 stone man with two fingers would somehow com-municate itself to the subject of the experiment?

At the present time, this question – like all the others raised in the present chapter – is unanswerable. The only thing that seems perfectly clear is that the 'other being' who inhabits Frankenstein's Castle is a miracle worker. His power to produce poltergeist effects is no more inherently surprising than his power to state confidently that a ten-digit number can be divided by 641 when there is no known mathematical shortcut to solving the problem. No doubt the reason he can perform these feats is that no one has ever explained to him that they are impossible.

# CHAPTER SIX

# Clues

THIS CHAPTER WILL be the most personal in the book. For it is now necessary to describe my own search for the 'other mode' of consciousness, and the major clues along the way. Parts of the story can be found in fragments in other books; but I want to try to tell it in logical sequence.

I suppose the most fundamental question you can ask of any human being is how far they are disposed to be an optimist or pessimist. I can conjure up the faces of certain children I know that seem permanently mournful, with the certainty that the grown-ups are in a conspiracy to deny them anything they really want. Others are naturally devil-may-care and cheerful, harbouring a serene confidence that life means well by them. Most are somewhere between the two. I was lucky in being born cheerful and confident. I was also lucky, I believe, in being born into a working-class background that came close to being 'deprived'. My father was a boot-and-shoe worker who seldom earned more than £3 a week during the '30s. We never went without food or clothes; but relative poverty meant a fairly dreary existence. So there was always plenty to struggle *for*. Films – and later books – told me that the world 'out there' was a vast and exciting place. I could hardly wait to grow up and start 'living'.

Not that I was ever over-confident. I have always been naturally introverted, and inclined to be over-sensitive about rebuffs and rejections. I seem to be a typical Cancer: obsessive, non-gregarious, deeply attached to my home. But these characteristics were always counterbalanced by a natural cheerfulness. Freud once said that a child who has been his mother's exclusive favourite carries through life a certain confidence of success. I was the first born in the family – my mother having got herself pregnant before any of her sisters, and obliged to hurry to the altar – so I was the favourite of the whole family. Unmarried aunts took me for walks and showed me off to their friends. Because I had long fingers, my mother was convinced that I would grow up to be a great pianist. (In fact, I have never showed the slightest talent for the piano.) From the beginning, everybody seemed to expect me to 'do well'. Although I never gave it any thought, I suppose I also came to take this for granted.

This notion of an immensely exciting world 'out there' tends to take the form of symbols. I think of tunnels of greenery, vast areas of dazzling flowers, and a sheet of water reflecting the sunlight. This image seems to date back to the age of two or three, when my father took me on his bicycle – he had made a little saddle that fitted on the crossbar – to the Abbey Park in Leicester. I have a feeling that life until that time had been cramped and dull; I have dim memories of kitchens smelling of greasy dishes, dark rooms with big plant pots in the window and tablecloths of dark-green baize with tassels. That day by the River Soar brought a sense of 'expectancy' – something like a sharp and delightful smell in the air. It is my first clear memory of the 'other mode'.

Christmas always brought it – together with a sense of reconciliation with the boredom of the rest of the year, the certainty that the bad times and the dull times were only the prelude to something more exciting. Again, it seems to be associated with an image or a mood – of snow, the smell of woodsmoke, the taste of custard and Christmas pudding, the silvery 'toys' on the artificial tree.

'Shades of the prison house' began to close in my early teens. But by that time I had discovered science, and worshipped Einstein and Eddington. So although the universe seemed colder and less magical, it was also bigger. I no longer daydreamed of being a cowboy or a famous song-and-dance man, but of inventing the atomic bomb or the first mechanical brain. That dream ended in 1945 with Hiroshima; but by then, my admiration for H. G. Wells had already convinced me that I might make a better novelist than a scientist. Besides, it seemed clear that the 'question' – of whether human existence has a meaning – is closer to the domain of the novelist than of the scientist. The discovery of Shaw at about this time – through the film of *Caesar and Cleopatra* and a radio production of *Man and Superman* – confirmed the decision to be what Shaw called an 'artist-philosopher'.

From the age of thirteen to the age of eighteen I did little but read and write. I was in a state of almost permanent depression, intensified by the need to work for a living from the age of sixteen. I worked as a warehouse clerk, a laboratory assistant and a civil servant. For the first time, some of the old confidence drained away, and I wondered if I would spend my life working at jobs I hated. A period of National Service in the RAF was at first a delightful change; but soon I detested it as much as the civil service. After six months I succeeded in getting myself thrown out – I have told the story at length elsewhere – and decided that I would prefer to be a tramp rather than waste any more time in offices and factories. My father was upset when I resigned my job as an established civil servant and threw me out of the house. I spent the next eighteen months wandering around England and France, taking casual jobs and often sleeping under hedges.

But by this time I had made my first important 'discovery'. A reference in T. S. Eliot – whom I admired more than any other writer except Shaw – led me to buy a copy of the *Bhagavad Gita*. Suddenly, the basic issue was clear to me. Man is a slave of his appetite and desires, of his 'personality'. Most of his misery is due to things he wants and can't have – women, fame, wealth. But what I had always enjoyed most was the world of ideas and the imagination. I had already learned how to place myself in a mental state of total relaxation and freedom through reading and poetry. And the world of poetry and ideas is free to anyone who has access to a public library. All that was necessary was to cultivate 'detachment'. I began to practise 'meditation', sitting cross-legged for hours, staring straight in front of me.

The result was a sudden and total transformation of my

inner-being. There was a sense of freedom from my personality – from the being called Colin Wilson who was born in
Leicester in 1931. I felt that 'he' was a series of responses and
reactions, of ambitions and frustrations. But after half an hour
of staring straight in front of me, of concentrating my
attention 'at the root of the eyebrows', I felt *in control* of his
responses and frustrations. This control brought such a sense
of exhilaration and satisfaction that I often sneaked away from
other people to spend just five minutes sitting cross-legged;
when I was working as a labourer on a building site, I would
find a quiet spot and, while the others were having a smoke,
would sit in a position that could quickly be changed to an
ordinary sitting posture if someone came by. . . .

At the age of twenty I got married – for the same reason
as my father – and the opportunities for meditation became
infrequent as I worked in a plastics factory to support my wife
and son. I had begun to study the Christian mystics –
Ruysbroek, Suso, St John of the Cross, even the spiritual
exercises of St Francis de Sales – and daydreamed of entering
a monastery. (The fact that I was not technically a Christian –
having rejected the idea that Jesus died for my sins – seemed
unimportant.) The marriage ended after two years and half a
dozen different homes (London landladies objected to babies),
and I thought even more seriously about entering a monastery,
even to the point of starting to receive instruction to become a
Catholic. But again I decided that I could never 'swallow' this
preposterous religion of sin and redemption. My religious
faith was closer to that of the Buddha or Vyasa (the mythical
author of the *Bhagavad Gita*): to cease to be a slave of human
desires and appetites. Besides, I have always enjoyed sex too
much to become a monk. (This was one appetite I was
prepared to live with.)

Soon after the break-up of my marriage, in 1953, I
decided to attempt to define this problem of the 'Outsider',
the man who feels detached from the society around him, and
who feels that most human beings are the slaves of self-
deception. I admired *The Brothers Karamazov* more than any
other novel; yet it seemed to me that its most important

section – Ivan's long conversation with Alyosha – misses the point. The real problem of human existence is not suffering, which is largely the outcome of human stupidity, laziness and self-deception. It is the question of whether human life is really meaningless and futile. Another Russian novelist, Artsybashev, had explored it in his novel *Breaking Point*, in which most of the characters in a dreary small town become convinced of the futility of their lives, and commit suicide. Suffering is admittedly one of the central problems of human existence; but this is because we have a suspicion that it is all *for nothing*. If we had a certainty about *meaning*, the suffering would be bearable. With no certainty of meaning, even comfort begins to seem futile. *Breaking Point* may be a bad novel; but Artsybashev had stated the real problem.

The problem ran like a thread through my own life. I had always wanted freedom – freedom from this dreary need to work for a living, freedom to live a life of the mind. Yet if I woke up in my room on a Saturday morning, with a whole weekend of 'freedom' in front of me, I might find myself trapped in a curious lukewarm state of indifference. Why does 'meaning' seem to vanish like a will-o'-the-wisp as soon as we have time to devote to it? Artsybashev believes that this is because meaning is an illusion created by problems and difficulties. . . .

If we had easy and continuous access to the 'other mode' of consciousness, it might be possible to answer the question of meaning, for we could place the two states side by side, so to speak, and decide between them.

I could recall those experiences of the 'other mode' in childhood, the alleyways of greenery, the snow and tinsel, the daydreams of glory. Therefore I was inclined to reject Artsybashev's nihilism. It seemed to me that Dostoevsky had come very close to the answer: once in *Crime and Punishment*, once in *The Brothers Karamazov*. In *Crime and Punishment*, Raskolnikov thinks that if he had to stand on a narrow ledge for ever and ever, in eternal darkness and tempest, he would still prefer to do that rather than die at once. In *The Brothers Karamazov*, Ivan tells the story of a sinner who had denied the after-life, and who was condemned by God to walk a billion miles. His first reaction is to lie on the ground for a thousand years or so and refuse to get up. Then, bored with this, he reluctantly carries out his sentence, dragging his feet every inch of the way. Finally, he completes the billion miles and is admitted into heaven – and says immediately that even five minutes in paradise would be worth walking another billion miles for. . . .

Dostoevsky had no doubt that the meaning is *realler* than the meaninglessness. In some odd sense, the meaninglessness is an illusion. Artsybashev's characters were fools to commit suicide. But how could they have *grasped* the meaning that would have saved them?

While I was writing *The Outsider*, I had an important insight, which I labelled 'the St Neot margin'. One hot, stuffy day in midsummer, I was hitch-hiking with my girlfriend – Joy – to see her parents in Peterborough. I had no desire to go; they wanted to know why we weren't getting married, and I felt it was none of their bloody business. (In fact, I was still un-divorced.) But I had no particular desire to stay in London either; I was working in another plastics factory with a foreman I disliked, and living in a remote suburb of North London. I felt bored and resentful. When a lorry stopped for us, I felt no particular gratitude. But after ten minutes or so, there was an ominous knocking sound from his engine. He said he would have to pull into the next garage; so we got out, thanked him, and plodded on. The road was deserted. Half an hour later, another lorry stopped. Still I felt no gratitude – just a feeling of: 'About time too . . .'

Ten minutes later, the odd coincidence occurred. There was a knocking noise from *his* engine. And, like the previous driver, he said he would have to pull in for repairs. This time I felt a wave of fury; fate was obviously playing tricks. At the same time, it struck me that this was the first positive feeling I had experienced that afternoon.

The driver found that if he dropped his speed down to twenty miles an hour, the knocking noise stopped; as soon as he accelerated, it started again. He was anxious to get to

Peterborough, and by this time, so was I. As we went through a
small town called St Neots, on the Huntingdon road, he said:
'I think if I keep to this speed, we'll probably make it.' I felt
a wave of exhilaration – followed by a sense of the absurdity of
it all. I thought: 'If someone had told me half an hour ago that
I would feel delighted to be sitting in the overheated cab of a
lorry, grinding along at twenty miles an hour, I would have
said he was mad . . .' So why *was* I so pleased? Because I had
been *threatened with inconvenience*, and the threat had been
withdrawn. It struck me that there is a state of consciousness,
an area of feeling, which is susceptible to stimulus by pain
or inconvenience, but not 'pleasant' events (i.e. I had felt no
pleasure when the lorry stopped to pick us up). Since we were
passing through St Neots at the time, I scrawled in my
notebook: 'St Neot margin' – meaning this margin – or
threshold – of negative stimulus. Then I forgot about it.
Several weeks later, I came across the note, and wondered
what the devil I'd meant by it. The words 'St Neot' gave me
the clue, and I reconstructed what had happened. And I
realised that it was one of the most important insights of my
life, and that I had come close to forgetting it.

For this *is* the problem – that harmless-looking state of
'disconnected' consciousness which drains all our strength
and sense of meaning. It is less spectacular than the Slough of
Despond, and therefore ten times as dangerous. It can easily
slip into full-blown schizophrenia. But it seems to be one of
the commonest states of human consciousness. I had experienced it simply out of lack of motivation – lack of desire to go
on to Peterborough, lack of desire to return to London. In
effect, it is a kind of doldrums, in which a ship lies becalmed
with slack sails. But this particular problem ceased to bother
sailors after someone invented the steam engine. Humankind
needs the psychological equivalent of the steam engine or the
internal combustion engine.

The next major insight came in the following year, 1954.
Again, I was with Joy – this time on holiday in the West
Country – where we subsequently came to live. I was now
living in a room in New Cross; Joy was working at a library in

Harrow, but spent weekends with me. Neither of us was in holiday mood, because Joy's menstrual period was late. The complications – if she were pregnant – would be enormous; she would have to give up work, we would have to find a flat together, I would have to start thinking about a job with a future. . . . The thought of the problems was depressing. On the second day of the holiday, we were walking along the seafront between Dawlish and Teignmouth; Joy vanished into the Ladies; then we walked on. We had walked several miles further when I said: 'We'll give it another day, then go back to London, and you'd better start taking hot baths . . .' She said casually: 'Oh, it's all right now . . .' It took several seconds for it to sink in; then I said: 'Do you mean to say . . . You idiot, why didn't you say so half an hour ago!' I was looking past her, across the sea, at the Exmouth peninsula. Suddenly, it struck me that it was immensely beautiful. I thought: 'No, it isn't – you're just feeling relieved.' Then I looked again, and thought: 'No. It *is* beautiful.' It struck me with amazement. For if this was – as I could now see – *objectively* beautiful, then my senses had been somehow *actively excluding* the beauty. And it was not simply worry that had caused it. If we had been on holiday with no problems, I would still have looked at the scenery wearing 'blinkers' – happy, perhaps, to be on holiday, but still not *seeing* what I could now see.

This story has a sequel. More than ten years later, Joy and I were living in Cornwall. In January 1966 I set out on a lecture tour of America. I detested the whole idea – I had been on a similar tour in 1961 and found it exhausting and repetitive – one-night stands in remote campuses, faculty parties, long drives to the nearest airport, then on to another campus, more 'unscheduled seminars', more faculty parties . . .

Depressed at the thought of spending three months away from my home and family – we now had two children – I had drunk too much wine the night before; so as I took my seat on the London train, I was suffering from a hangover. The thought of all those students, all those faculty parties ('What do you think of America?'), all those little country airports ('Welcome to Wilkes-Barre') plunged me into something like despair; I was already sick of America, and I hadn't even reached London Airport.

It was a grey, warm January day, and the train was too hot. I sat alone in my compartment and stared gloomily out of the window. An intuition told me that this disgust was *dangerous* – that this was Dylan Thomas's state of mind on his final lecture tour. As the train passed the bridge over the River Teign, and Babbacombe Bay came into sight, I recalled that day in 1954 when I had experienced such relief. I went out into the corridor and opened the window; the train passed the actual spot on the beach where Joy had told me she wasn't pregnant. I looked at it, then across at the Exmouth peninsula, and thought: 'This is absurd. I saw that it *is* beautiful. Yet now I can't see it again.' I went back into the carriage, stared out of the window, and suddenly felt a kind of rage. It was stupid that I should be unable to see something I knew to be there. I clenched my teeth and concentrated. I stared at the scenery until my face went red – anybody looking at me would have thought I was having a heart attack. Then, suddenly, it happened. There was an immense feeling of relief, and a sense of some interior 'opening', as if enormous doors had slowly slid back. Suddenly, I could see it again – the almost incredible beauty of everything I looked at.

I maintained the state of insight all the way to London. In America, I declined to allow myself to become bored; if I had a two-hour wait at an airport, I spent it writing or thinking, or just doing 'concentration exercises'. Only in the final week of the tour did the exhaustion slip past my guard – and I instantly became accident-prone. Everything went wrong. But a week later I was back in England – tired, but still, on the whole, in good spirits.

This story also has a sequel. Later that year, I had to travel to London on the overnight train to see a film producer. There was a breakdown on the line, and the train arrived in Paddington several hours late. I drove straight to the producer's hotel – without time to eat breakfast – and drank a whisky while we talked. A couple of hours later, I was back on the train – very tired, and with a slight headache. The thought of the five-hour return journey bored me. I had no desire to read, and I no longer felt like eating. Then I remembered what had happened in January, and decided to try it again. As the train pulled out of Paddington, I stared out of the window, and concentrated until I went red in the face. Within a minute or less, it had happened again – the same feeling of inner-doors grinding open, and an enormous relief. But this time, there was a difference, due to my tiredness. All the colours of the scenery became soft and blurred; the greens took on a gentle tinge of blue. And in some odd way, the scenery seemed to *hold* my eyes – I could only liken the sensation to walking through dry thistles and feeling those tiny hooks catching in your clothes, trying to hold you back. Everything seemed suffused with a delicious melancholy. And again, I was amazed to realise that a determined mental effort could transform the texture of consciousness. In effect, I had achieved the same 'break-through' as Jane Wolfe, after Crowley made her sit for three weeks looking at the sea; but I did it in about a minute.

I had, in fact, grasped the fundamental mechanism of such experiences many years before. When I was nineteen, I worked in the office of a steelworks in Leicester; after a week or so, I had sunk into a state of glassy-eyed boredom. And as I walked around the works, carrying memoranda from the office, watching molten steel pouring out of a furnace, I would be aware that the trouble lay in the *automatic* part of consciousness. My dislike of the job made my mind·*switch off* as soon as I arrived at work. The mere smell of the office was like a hypnotist snapping his fingers, and I went into a kind of trance. I called it the 'automatic pilot'. Years later I preferred to call it the 'robot'. Any sudden crisis or emergency will cause us to snap out of robotic consciousness. This is what happened to Graham Greene's 'whiskey priest' as he stood in front of the firing squad.

What I had discovered is that a sudden intense mental effort is just as effective as a firing squad for dismissing the robot.

Another experience of the 1960s underlined the point.

I had spent several days in my home town, Leicester, much of it in pubs with my father. When I set out to drive back to Cornwall – one afternoon about two o'clock – I was drowsy from the beer consumed at lunch-time, and suffering from what I call 'people poisoning' – too much social intercourse. I was too tired to enjoy the drive; my only thought was to get back home and spend twenty-four hours listening to music . . .

Our route took us through Cheltenham, where I knew there was a good second-hand bookshop; I decided to stop there. We arrived at about half-past four, and parked about ten yards from the shop. I went in, with my three-year-old daughter Sally, while Joy began rearranging the luggage in the boot to make room for books. . . . After five minutes in the shop, Sally grew bored, and asked: 'Where's mummy?' I took her to the door of the shop, and pointed at Joy, who was still rummaging in the boot. Then I went back to the books. Five minutes later, Joy came into the shop alone. Several minutes went by before I asked casually: 'Where's Sally?' Joy said: 'I thought you had her.' There was instant panic. We both rushed out into the street. It was now the rush-hour, and the road was jammed with traffic. There was no sign of Sally. Joy went one way and I went the other. Twenty yards further on, I came to a large intersection with traffic lights and a pedestrian barrier; it was obvious that she could not have gone that way. I turned and went back. Joy was outside the shop; she had also stopped at a crowded intersection and decided Sally had not gone that way.

By this time I was desperate. We had never been separated from Sally for a minute since she had been born; now she had vanished. I had to master a rising sense of misery and disaster. Obviously, it would do no good to give way to panic or self-pity; what was needed was simply a determination to find her – if it took the next twenty-four hours.

When I went back to the shop the next time, Joy had found her. She had wandered round the corner, and was on the other side of the block. At least she had stayed on the pavement. I bought the books I had chosen and got into the car. I have never experienced such relief. Again, I noticed how beautiful everything looked. A bus that held us up at a traffic light seemed a delightful object; even exhaust smoke struck me as a pleasant smell.

What was important here, I believe, was not my relief, but the fact that I had refused to give way to panic, and had 'summoned energy' to meet the emergency. The result was that, as I drove along a crowded road through the drizzle, I felt no impatience – only enormous gratitude that everything should be so *interesting*.

In each of these cases, I observed that the trouble began with a feeling of boredom *and resentment*. I had resented having to go to Peterborough to see Joy's parents; I had resented having to go to America to lecture. In each case, it was as if something inside me had groaned 'Oh *no!*', and refused to go any further.

Again, it was something I had known about for years. When I was thirteen, I took my younger brother out one Sunday afternoon for a long cycle ride; we went much further than intended, and were still ten miles from home when dusk arrived. My brother had never been that far from home without an adult; I could see how much strain he was under. We had no bicycle lamps with us, and on the Market Harborough road, a policeman stopped us and told us we would have to walk. He obviously had no intention of forcing us to walk to Leicester, for he rode off in the opposite direction. We got back on our bicycles. Suddenly, my brother turned his front wheel into the grass verge, flung himself down, and began to cry. I happened to be looking at him as he did this, and I saw him *decide* to do it. He was not suddenly overwhelmed with misery and panic; he decided that it was time to 'give in'. (After five minutes, he cheered up and we got home without further mishap.) He felt that fate was treating him badly; his reaction was to refuse to go on.

Years later, I observed my other brother reacting in the same way. I had taken him on holiday to the Lake District, and we climbed Helvellyn. I underestimated the distance; hours later, when we staggered out on to the Ullswater road, it was dark; it had also started to rain. We walked up over the

Kirkstone Pass; finally, a car gave us a lift back to our camping site above Windermere. It was midnight, and we were both soaked and cold. I made hot soup. My brother drank it; but he refused to remove his wet clothes. He was feeling a generalised resentment – not against me, but against 'life', for demanding such an unreasonable effort from an eleven-year-old boy. So in going to sleep in wet clothes, he was trying to get his own back – as if saying: 'If I wake up with pneumonia, it will be your fault.' Like Ivan Karamazov, he was offering God back his entrance ticket – or at least, registering a protest. Fortunately, we both woke up feeling fine. Again, I noted the curious irrationality of human resentment.

In 1973, I had another chance to observe it in myself; during a period of heavy overwork, I began to experience a series of 'panic attacks' in the middle of the night. I have described this in the opening pages of *Mysteries*, so I shall not do so here, except to say that the attacks brought a feeling of rising panic, like milk boiling over in a saucepan. I was afraid that my heart would accelerate until it stopped. Gradually, I learned how to control them, by waking myself up as fully as possible – in effect, calling upon a more 'adult' level of myself to restore order. But the chief lesson of the attacks was that a 'childish' level of me was revolting against all the overwork, and various other strains and problems. It was groaning: 'Oh *no!*' The result was 'negative feedback' between the two halves of the brain, and a plunge into a feeling of total 'mistrust'.

It took just one more panic attack to bring this lesson home to me. It happened in 1978, when I was on my way to lecture at the Edinburgh Festival. It had been more than ten years since I had been in Scotland, and our two youngest children had never been there; so it seemed a good idea to combine the lecture trip with our annual holiday. We drove up, and stopped for the weekend in a hotel at Ullswater.

The weather had become overcast and rather chilly. On Sunday afternoon, we took the children on the lake steamer to Pooley Bridge, and walking in the woods; on the way back the weather suddenly became chilly; we arrived back at the hotel cold and tired. I dragged myself down to dinner, but felt more like sleeping than eating; back in my room, I fell asleep immediately. I woke up in the middle of the night, sweating and feeling sick. The room was far too hot – the hotel seemed to have switched on its central heating in early September. I began thinking about Scotland, and decided that I didn't want to go; the thought of grey skies and rain-drenched moors was depressing. I felt a wave of the same 'reluctance' that I had experienced on the way to America in 1966. Suddenly, my heartbeat began to accelerate, and I felt myself sinking into a whirlpool of nausea. I got out of bed, went and splashed cold water on my face in the bathroom, then sat on the lavatory, concentrating hard, trying to soothe the panic. After a few minutes, I succeeded; the nausea – both physical and mental – vanished, and I felt a wave of relief.

Back in bed I analysed what had happened, and saw the answer quite clearly. It was that sudden sense of 'Oh no!' that had started the landslide into 'panic'. In effect, I had tried to abdicate. And that is as dangerous as the driver of a car suddenly deciding that he wants to sleep.

At breakfast the next morning, I could see the solution: *never* to be tempted to give way to that sense of defeat. In two words: never retreat. Mental breakdown, I am convinced, is always a kind of landslide into defeat. We have been battling – more or less successfully – against various problems; now, suddenly, it all seems too much. Life seems futile. Quite suddenly, one's whole mental superstructure collapses into pessimism, like a demolished building. *That* is what mental illness is about.

In my case, I could see that such pessimism was absurd. I had fought my battles against 'nihilism' in my teens. Intellectually, I *knew* beyond all shadow of doubt that the 'vision of meaning' is true, and that the nausea is a lie. Therefore, these panic attacks were a kind of misunderstanding – in effect, a surrender to the pessimism of the right-brain. (Sperry noted that the left-brain seems to be basically optimistic, the right pessimistic.) It was my own fault for allowing myself to give way to that sudden feeling of 'reluctance'.

All that was necessary was to 'pull myself together', to deliberately pour energy and enthusiasm into the trip to Scotland. Never retreat. At breakfast that morning I told myself this was the real solution. Ever since then, the certainty has deepened.

I have talked so far of personal experiences. But a few other 'clues', equally important, were learned from other people.

In the early 1960s, I became friendly with Robert Ardrey, the author of *African Genesis*. Ardrey had a genius for collecting essential items of information about human and animal behaviour. It was he who told me that precisely 5 per cent of any species is 'dominant', and that this figure is strangely constant. The Chinese made this discovery during the Korean war, when they tried separating the dominant American prisoners – the inveterate 'escapers' – from the others, and found that, once the escapers had been confined separately, the remainder could be left with almost no guards, and no one tried to escape. The escapers were always one in twenty – 5 per cent.

The mental 'escapers' are also members of that 5 per cent – the human beings who revolt against the confinement of everyday consciousness. These are the 'Outsiders'. The others find it hard to understand what makes them so dissatisfied. (This no doubt explains why my own books have never reached a wide audience, and probably never will.)

Ardrey told me another story that brought an even deeper insight: the story of the 'double ambiguity' planaria.

A planarion worm, or flatworm, is one of the most rudimentary of living creatures, with no stomach or rectum, and virtually no brain. Like laboratory rats, they are an invaluable tool of research.

In 1958, two zoologists named Rubinstein and Best were

trying to find out how planaria can learn – in spite of the absence of a brain, and they devised a simple experiment to demonstrate this learning ability. The worms were placed in a plastic tube containing water – they need water to live. Then a tap was turned so the water drained from the tube. In a panic, the worms rushed off down the tube looking for water; soon they encountered a fork. One way was lighted and led to water; the other way was dark, and didn't. Soon, most of the planaria had learned to find water by choosing the lighted branch.

But as Rubinstein and Best continued to repeat the experiment, an odd thing happened. The planaria suddenly began choosing the wrong alleyway. After more trials, they simply lay still and refused to move, as if saying: 'Oh God, not again!' They actually preferred to die rather than go in search of water.

It seemed that they had got bored as the sense of emergency wore off. But how could a creature without a brain get bored? Rubinstein and Best devised a more complicated experiment. This time they used two tubes; one was made of rough plastic inside, the other of smooth, so the planaria could feel the difference with their undersides. In the rough tube, the water was down the lighted alleyway; in the other, it was down the dark one. They took a new lot of planaria, and started all over again.

This was a far more difficult task, and only a small proportion – about a third – of the worms learned to find the water in either tube. But that third never regressed. They never chose the wrong alleyway, or lay down and died. They had been forced to put far more effort into the learning process. The result was that they never got bored. They never groaned and said: 'Oh no!'

This story struck me as a revelation. The second lot of worms had simply *doubled* their effort. They forced themselves to go beyond the 'Oh no!' point. And they ceased to be subject to 'life failure', defeat-proneness, the desire to turn their back on a challenge.

I had stumbled upon the same trick on my way to

America in 1966. The prospect of all those American students
made me want to turn my back on the whole thing. I simply
made a conscious effort to put twice as much energy into the
challenge. As a result, I enjoyed the tour.

But then, a flatworm, unlike a human being, does not
have a double brain. It consists of only two parts: 'instinctive'
drive, and a 'robot'. The robot soon learned to guide them to
water. But instinctive drive was not enough to stimulate them
to repeat the process indefinitely. So they died.

That is the trouble with instinct. It is powerful, but
*short-sighted*. When their instinctive 'self' became bored with
finding water, they became overwhelmed with a sense of
discouragement. On the train to London, I simply *overruled*
my instinctive self; the result was a successful adjustment to
the challenge.

Clearly, this is why the force of evolution decided that
a left-brain is necessary. That simple combination of instinct
and robot can be a disaster. The robot was created for the
storage of learning. But if the learning is achieved too easily,
then the robot becomes a liability instead of an advantage,
advising you to accept defeat rather than redouble your effort.
In effect, it is telling you that 'it just isn't worth it'. I had seen
the same mechanism operating in my brothers.

This is why we need the left-brain ego: to overrule
instinct and the robot. These two form a purely mechanical
alliance. Instinct assesses the urgency of a situation, the robot
places that judgement on permanent record, and from then
on, decides whether a certain effort is *worth* making. And the
danger here is not simply that the resulting alliance can make
us choose death rather than greater effort – this, after all, is a
rarity. It is that the alliance keeps us *trapped* at a certain level
of mechanicalness. It tells me that the day ahead of me is
going to be fairly uninteresting, and that therefore I need
make no particular effort. A single glimpse of crisis, or a flash
of sudden joy, tells me that *no* day is uninteresting, that the
next half hour might be the most important of my life. We are
stupid to waste our lives in mechanical repetition. To the
right-brain, the words 'Nothing to do' mean boredom; to the

left, they mean freedom. A third member of the alliance was necessary to rescue the other two from mechanicalness.

And this observation in itself has astounding implications. For what is abundantly obvious is that *we seldom use the left-brain for that purpose.* We may have developed the left-brain to rescue us from the defeat of the planaria. *Yet it has not rescued us.* We treat the left-brain ego as a useful adviser. But few of us really trust it. When the chips are down, we prefer to rely on instinct and the robot. And so, like the planaria, we lie down and die. And, what is worse, we waste our lives.

# CHAPTER SEVEN

# Discoveries

TOWARDS THE END of *The Law of Psychic Phenomena*, Hudson made these extraordinary statements:

1. The subjective mind exercises complete control over the functions and sensations of the body.
2. The subjective mind is amenable to control by the suggestions of the objective mind.
3. These two propositions being true, the conclusion is obvious, that the functions and sensations of the body can be controlled by the suggestions of the objective mind.

Hudson died in 1903. In a sense, he was lucky. The current of the age was now flowing powerfully against him. The ideas of Freud were crossing the water from Europe. If Freud had ever heard of Hudson's 'three principles', he would have dismissed them as a typical example of human self-deception and *hubris*, based upon total failure to appreciate the truth about the Unconscious. According to Freud, the 'objective mind' (or personal consciousness) has *no* power – not even the ordinary power we take for granted: to make logical decisions. It is the subjective mind – the Unconscious – that really makes the decisions. Consciousness is a helpless puppet.

But then, Freud was so hostile to what he called 'the black tide of occultism' that he would never have dreamed of opening a book called *The Law of Psychic Phenomena*. He made no secret of his emotional rejection of such matters. The nearest he ever came to discussing them was in a paper called 'Psychoanalysis and Telepathy' (1921). There he remarks that he had intended to write about a case of 'a patient of a special kind, who discussed in his analytic hour matters which were related in a striking manner to an experience of my own immediately before his hour'. But he goes on to say that, on looking for his notes on the case, he finds he has brought along the wrong sheet of paper. 'Nothing is to be done in the face of so obvious a resistance.' So we shall probably never learn the details of the 'case of the special patient'.

The discovery of the fundamental difference between the left and right cerebral hemispheres was the beginning of a turn of the tide. To begin with, there seems to be little doubt that the right-brain *is* 'the Unconscious'. It behaves exactly like the Freudian unconscious; the author of a recent book on split-brain research boldly entitles a chapter on the right-brain 'The "Unconscious Mind" Discovered'.* No doubt other parts of the brain – like the cerebellum – play an equally important part in our unconscious activities. But for all practical purposes, we shall not go far wrong if we treat 'unconscious' as a synonym for 'right-brain'.

In which case, Freud's sinister picture of the unconscious as a mouldering cellar full of rats and centipedes, or an ocean full of squids and sharks, is quite simply a libel on that invaluable and highly creative area of the brain. It is true that the right is more pessimistic than the left, so that patients with left-brain damage are more inclined to emotion – especially negative emotion – than patients with right-brain damage. But that is simply because feeling is more short-sighted than thought, and therefore inclined to over-react to minor problems. Fundamentally, the right-brain has a job to do – like the left – and it gets on with it in the same down-to-earth and practical manner. The brain may be a Frankenstein's Castle, but we shall not find any mad monsters lurking in its cellars.

More than half a century after the death of Thomson J. Hudson, an American doctor named Howard Miller began to think his way towards the same basic principles. Like Hudson, Miller began by being intrigued by the phenomena

* *The Right Brain*, A New Understanding of the Unconscious Mind and Its Creative Powers, by Thomas R. Blakesee, London 1980.

of hypnosis. One of his patients urgently needed dental treatment, but could not stand injections. Miller read about a dentist who used hypnosis and decided it would be worth trying. He watched the dentist place his patient in a hypnotic trance. And at this point, he was staggered to hear the dentist ordering the patient not to bleed when the tooth was extracted. This seemed preposterous. How can the mind control bleeding? Yet when the tooth had been extracted, no blood came out of the cavity.

But if hypnosis can control bleeding, why not other physical problems – like cancer? Miller tried it, and the results amazed him. Two of his patients had breast tumours, one malignant, one benign. Miller was, in fact, treating them for other problems – one had an ulcer, the other asthma. Under hypnotic treatment, the benign tumour vanished completely, while the malignant one shrank to a quarter of its size. Two women with cancer of the cervix improved dramatically under hypnosis, although neither was totally cured. But a man suffering from high blood pressure and Lupus Erythamatosus – an unpleasant skin eruption – reacted to hypnotic treatment with a return to normal blood pressure, followed, a month later, by total disappearance of the skin problem. Miller tried the same treatment on patients with high cholesterol, steroids and blood sugar, and found they could also be reduced back to normal. Two women suffering from uterine bleeding – which was not responding to normal therapy – were soon reacting to suggestions of normal bleeding and clotting with complete disappearance of the symptoms.

But *what* was causing the cure? The answer was obvious. The *thought* of the hypnotist was somehow affecting the 'involuntary nervous system', demonstrating that it is not as involuntary as had been assumed. Which led Miller to the startling – and totally heretical – conclusion that the control centre of the involuntary nervous system may lie in the cerebral cortex. 'The pituitary and hypothalamus are thought to be the control centres of the involuntary nervous and glandular systems. However, there also exist many neuro-circulatory hormones secreted by the cerebral cortex itself. These hormones directly affect the hypothalamus as well as the pituitary – thus suggesting *that the cerebral cortex itself* is the true control centre of the hormonal and nervous systems.'*

But this was only a beginning. What startled Miller was this notion that *thought itself* could cause the change. In a paper called 'What is Thought?',† Miller took a significant step further. It seems to me perhaps the most significant step that has been taken by the science of psychology in the twentieth century.

Hypnosis, says Miller, is obviously based on thought and its power to influence the mind and body. But what *is* thought? The usual answer is that thought is the 'content' of the brain – its words and symbols and pictures. But supposing, said Miller, that thought is not *generated* by the brain? Suppose it only works *through* it, using the brain – and in turn the body – as a tool?

Expressed in this way, the notion sounds – admittedly – preposterous. After all, thought is usually recognised to be the *act* of thinking. We may agree with the behaviourists that this act is performed by the brain; or we may choose to believe that man has some kind of 'self' that presides over consciousness and directs the act of thinking. But it is difficult to see how thought itself can do the thinking.

In fact, it soon becomes clear that Miller believes in the 'presiding self' theory of mental activity. Close your eyes, he says, and observe the mental activities that go on inside your head – it is almost like watching a television screen. But *who* is looking at the screen? The answer, he says, is an 'internal observer' whom he prefers to call the 'Unit of Pure Thought'.

During brain surgery operations, Wilder Penfield would first of all apply tiny electric currents to various parts of the brain to locate the area responsible for epileptic seizures. The patient remained wide awake (the brain has no feeling). The patients often experienced detailed 'playbacks' of long-forgotten memories – as detailed as a video-tape recording.

---

* *Emotions and Malignancy*, a paper presented at the American Society of Clinical Hypnosis, San Francisco, Nov. 1, 1969.
† Presented to American Society of Clinical Hypnosis, Oct. 1971.

Sometimes it was exactly like dreaming while wide awake (a technique that Jung called 'active imagination').

Clearly, the brain is a giant computer, an information-storage system. We recognise this when a tune runs in our heads and we can't get it out. Yet we also make a natural, unexamined assumption that the brain is 'me', the 'real me'. When I dream, some other part of 'me' pours its startling fantasies and images on to the television screen inside my head. So I am inclined to feel that the 'conscious me' is an inferior part of something far more strange and complex. This is, of course, the classic Freudian view.

Miller is denying this theory. He is saying that the 'real you' is that internal observer. If you close your eyes and conjure up a certain idea or image, this internal observer has *given the order* a split-second before the image appears. It may be true that the computer chatters on, filling our heads with irrelevant ideas, images and tunes. But the 'real you', the Unit of Pure Thought, is the boss.

And that takes us right to the heart of the matter. For our problem is that *he doesn't know he is*. Miller says: 'Not knowing this previously, we mistakenly believed that the mental forms were "what we were thinking" rather than realising that they are only images *being observed*. Lack of this awareness has kept us from picking up the reins and taking control of our own brains. Not knowing who is the real master, we allowed our own inner movie storage projector to run its film haphazardly. It was able to dominate us because we believe that the mental forms constituted our thoughts, and therefore, we identified with and acted on them – as *thought precedes all action*. Our resultant behaviour, our reaction, was based therefore, for the most part, on phantasmagoria. The combination storage-movie projector should not and does not have to run wild. There should be and there is a projectionist, a controller, in attendance.'

The catch, of course, being that he does not realise that he is the controller. He thinks he is merely a helpless spectator. He sits on a chair in the corner of the room, watching the confused movie on the screen and wondering why it is so nonsensical, totally failing to recognise that *he* ought to' be 'in charge'.


Let me admit that, when Miller first sent me his two papers – both of them amounting to no more than a few hundred words – I at first failed to grasp the significance of his tremendous insight. It seemed to me that Miller had simply stumbled upon a discovery that had been made by Edmund Husserl more than half a century ago – that there *is* a 'transcendental ego' which presides over consciousness. Husserl was contradicting the theory of consciousness held by David Hume, in which consciousness is merely an association of ideas and feelings – in other words, the film running without a projectionist. Sartre had preferred to go back to Hume's view of consciousness without a transcendental ego, and I had pointed out his error in the mid-1960s.

Now in a sense, I was correct. Miller *had* rediscovered Husserl's transcendental ego, which he called the Unit of Pure Thought. But his revolutionary contribution is his recognition that this ego is in a thorough state of confusion, failing to grasp that it *ought* to be in charge.

The realisation dawned on me some months later. This is how it came about. One afternoon, after spending a long day at the typewriter, I decided to take the dogs for a walk on the cliffs. The trouble with these late afternoon walks is that I find it difficult to unwind. The scenery is beautiful, yet if I try to relax and enjoy it, I find myself merely thinking about the problems I have been writing about. My left-brain has been churning out words all day, and I am stuck in left-brain consciousness, which is basically feelingless. (Extreme left-brain awareness is the same thing as schizophrenia – a condition in which everything seems unreal.)

But I can, in fact, relax by making a powerful mental effort of concentration – analogous to pointing a gun at my head and pulling the trigger. This has the effect of causing the right-brain to snap out of its state of semi-hypnotic passivity.

Suddenly, the scenery becomes 'real', and I begin to experience 'feedback' from my surroundings.

As I strolled along, I recalled Graham Greene's description of how he 'snapped himself out' of a state of near-schizophrenia by playing Russian roulette with his brother's revolver. What is the precise *mechanism* of this 'awakening'?

Then I saw the answer. The right-brain has fallen asleep, bored by the endless verbalising of the left. But in emergency, the left-brain shouts: 'Wake up!' And the right obeys.

That conclusion left me slightly stunned. It was not quite what I had been expecting. We have become so conditioned to thinking of the 'intellectual ego' as a villain that I found my explanation disturbing. Surely, the correct answer should be: the transcendental ego – some 'higher self' that presides over consciousness?

Yet the more I thought about it, the more inescapable seemed my conclusion: that the 'controller' of consciousness is – quite simply – the left-brain ego, Hudson's 'objective mind'.

Now I recalled Howard Miller's paper on the Unit of Pure Thought. When I arrived home, I dug it out of my file and re-read it. This time it came as a revelation. It is true that Miller's Unit of Pure Thought is Husserl's Transcendental Ego – subsequent correspondence with him has left me in no doubt about that. What is so important about his paper is his insight into the *cause* of the confusion – that, trapped in its narrow conceptual consciousness, overawed by the enormous mechanisms of the brain and body, the 'presiding ego' fails to realise that it ought to be in control. So it sits in a corner, studying the feelings and sensations of the body, and waiting to be told what to do.

I compared the situation to a couple of Irish navvies who have been sent out to dig a trench; but each one is under the impression that the other is the foreman. So they keep glancing at one another, waiting for orders. One picks up his shovel; the other thinks this is a hint that he ought to start work, and spits on his hands. The other thinks this is a hint that he ought to do the same, and puts down his shovel again. . . . And so the confusion continues.

Only in emergencies does the presiding ego remember that it ought to be in charge. In a story called *Soldier's Home*, which I quote in *The Outsider*, Hemingway describes a soldier back from the war, feeling utterly bored and lost in his home town. When he tells people about his war experiences, they somehow seem untrue, as if he is inventing them. Yet he can recall his immediate response to emergency and danger, 'all the times that had been able to make him feel cool and clear inside him when he thought about them; the times when he had done the one thing, the only thing for a man to do, easily and naturally, when he might have done something else . . .'.

Now I thought about it, I saw that this explained my own experiences of responding to problems or emergencies. In that lorry on the way to Peterborough, I had felt no desire to see Joy's parents; therefore, the presiding ego had abdicated in disgust, and the right-brain, deprived of a sense of direction, was yawning with boredom. It took the coincidence of that second breakdown – or near-breakdown – to make the presiding ego rouse itself with a groan of 'Oh no!' Then, as it concentrated on the sound of the engine, the right also woke up. Stan aroused himself from his slumbers. And when the driver said: 'I think we're going to make it', both burst into cheers.

The same with the experience of losing Sally in Cheltenham. 'I' was convinced that I was exhausted after several days of drinking and socialising too much, so 'I' left the robot to drive the car while I stared gloomily at the passing scenery and wished I was back home. Again, Stan fell asleep. When I realised we had lost her, I experienced a momentary temptation to give way to negative emotion – which would have been pointless; then 'I' dismissed it and took control, determined to treat this as a problem to which I could find a solution. The 'mystical' sense of reality as we drove on was not due to relief at finding her; it was 'primal perception', with the presiding ego in charge and the right-brain wide awake and doing its proper work of *supporting* consciousness. Boredom is 'unsupported' consciousness.

During those panic attacks of 1973, I had arrived at the

conclusion that we all contain a 'ladder of selves', a whole 'hierarchy' of personalities, and that this probably explains the phenomenon of multiple personality. When I learned to control the attacks – during the night – by waking myself up as fully as possible, it seemed to me that I was calling upon a higher level of the hierarchy – that I was, in effect, making an immense effort to drag myself up to the next rung of the ladder. This image still strikes me as basically valid; our personal evolution proceeds in steps which resemble a ladder. But all I was actually doing was to shout 'Enough of this nonsense', and taking control.

So why do we feel so naturally suspicious of such a conclusion: that the 'boss' ought to give orders and see that they are obeyed? To begin with, because it seems rather dangerous. Surely, this complex of body and brain and feelings ought to be a democracy in which everyone is allowed to have his say? When I feel tired or ill, I 'listen' to my body. When I feel worried, I listen to my feelings. When I feel love or pity, I listen to my emotions. This seems all very right and proper. To say that the left-brain ego ought to be 'in charge' seems almost tantamount to fascism, a dictator state.

But is this quite true? My body and my emotions tell me *lies*. If I have been writing all day, and I feel I ought to get some exercise, my body assures me that I am tired. And indeed, I may have to force it to go for a walk, like a reluctant horse. But if I happen to meet an old friend on my walk, and we get into an absorbing conversation, the fatigue vanishes. My body was 'shamming'. And if I am feeling tired, and I recollect that I have to take part in a television programme tomorrow, I experience a 'sinking feeling' and a desire to find an excuse to call it off. In fact, once in the studio, the 'reluctance' vanishes and I begin to enjoy it. My feelings were 'shamming'. And, by ignoring them, I am practising a mild form of the 'bullying treatment' which, according to William James, could cure 'neurasthenic' patients. 'First comes the very extremity of distress, then follows unexpected relief.' And James goes on: 'There seems to be no doubt that *we are each and all of us to some extent victims of habit-neurosis* . . . We live subject to arrest by degrees of fatigue which we have come only from habit to obey. Most of us can learn to push the barrier further off, and to live in perfect comfort on much higher levels of power.' So, in fact, most of us are like a backward country which has learned to live with a high level of inefficiency and corruption. A little genuine authority can only be an improvement.

There is another argument that sounds far more persuasive, and it is presented in its most effective form by D. H. Lawrence. This points out that the personal ego tends to be narrow and stupid and obsessive, and that all 'mystical revelations' are due to a dissolution of the ego. In one of his poems, Lawrence tells a woman:

> And be, oh be
> A sun to me,
> Not a weary, importunate
> Personality.

And the majority of his novels and stories are about people who learn to abandon the 'weary, importunate personality' to something bigger and more universal, sex, primitive instinct, even (in one story) the sun itself. His novels are also full of characters – like Gerald Crich in *Women in Love* who could be called 'will-worshippers', and who usually come to a nasty end.

But no one would deny that the left-brain can be neurotic and obsessive. William James says: 'Compared to what we ought to be, we are only half awake. . . . In some persons this sense of being cut off from their rightful resources is extreme, and we get the formidable neurasthenic and psychasthenic conditions, with life grown into one tissue of impossibilities. . . .' And our 'rightful resources' are those hidden powers of the right. *These* are what Lawrence's 'will-worshippers' have cut themselves off from.

But how do we re-establish contact with these powers? It is true that we may 'abandon' ourselves to sex or nature or 'instinct'. But what happens in all moments of sudden joy or deep insight is a magnificent sense of *control*. It happens if you set out on holiday, and suddenly find yourself appreciating the green of the trees and the feel of the wind on your face. *You are again in control.* Our real problem is that neurotic tendency of the left-ego to isolate itself from the powers of the right, and then to *forget* that those powers are at its disposal; this is James's feeling of 'being separated from our rightful resources'.

The word 'forget' offers us the real key to the situation. Man's evolution over the past four or five thousand years has been due to his determination *not* to forget. Animals are always forgetting. Nietzsche said that we envy the cows their happiness, but it is no use asking them the secret of happiness, because they have forgotten the question before they can give an answer. Man developed language to help him store knowledge, then went on to invent writing. The outcome was modern civilisation. He has even learned to store non-verbal knowledge. The sculptures of Michelangelo are an example; so are the symphonies of Beethoven. Yeats wrote:

> Michael Angelo left a proof
> On the Sistine Chapel roof,
> Where but half-awakened Adam
> Can disturb globe-trotting Madam
> Till her bowels are in a heat,
> Proof that there's a purpose set
> Before the secret working mind:
> Profane perfection of mankind.

Somehow, Michelangelo can express the fundamental purpose of mankind without words; yet his figures still shout aloud.

But although art is a powerful means of 'reminding' us of the powers of the right-brain self, it is not the solution we are looking for. In his novel *Buddenbrooks*, Thomas Mann describes the seaside holidays on which young Hanno Buddenbrook is taken by his family. Hanno is an artist by temperament; he is bored by school, and loves the seaside. Yet the family doctor observes that he seems to be *weakened* by his holidays. His ecstatic 'surrender' to nature intensifies his dislike of the commercial city where he lives, lowering his powers of resistance. Art can have much the same effect – this was the problem of so many 'Outsiders' of the nineteenth century; their sensitivity 'unmanned' them and made them unfit for the business of everyday living. In fact, the problem is really one of insufficient exposure. If Hanno had spent two months at the seaside instead of two weeks, he would have been made stronger, not weaker. On the same principle, you feel stronger after a good night's sleep; but if you were shaken awake after half an hour's sleep, you would feel weak and confused. Unfortunately, the Beethovens and Michelangelos – the artistic equivalent of a good night's sleep – are rarities. This is why art is an unsatisfactory solution.

But then, Hudson and Miller have provided us with the real basis for a solution. Both seem to be in agreement that the *power* lies in the hands of the 'subjective mind', but that this mind is subject to control by the presiding ego – the objective mind or Unit of Pure Thought. Hudson even states that all the functions and sensations of the body should be controllable by the objective mind.

The prospect sounds marvellous. But *how*?

Consider again what happens when I experience sudden 'delight', the feeling of freshness and 'newness', the sense of 'primal perception'. It also happens, as D. H. Lawrence points out, in the sexual orgasm. The 'delight' is accompanied by an insight, which could be defined as the recognition that life is infinitely richer and more interesting than I had given it credit for.

Such direct perception provides me with the most powerful kind of purpose. Our problem is defeat-proneness, lack of purpose. If we could have this kind of perception all the time, the problem would vanish.

But this kind of 'primal perception' is rare. It certainly plays a small part in our sense of purpose. This usually operates in a more roundabout manner. Consider the story told by the psychiatrist Viktor Frankl about his days as a prisoner in a concentration camp. A large number of prisoners had been sent from Auschwitz to Dachau; they were kept standing four hours in the rain, frozen and half-starved. Yet, says Frankl, they were all laughing and joking – because Dachau had no chimney.

What has happened is that the left-brain has recognised that the absence of a chimney means absence of a crematorium; it has passed on this information to the right-brain, which recognises that it means life instead of death. The right-brain responds with a surge of energy. The whole process is *symbolic*. The right is responding to the *suggestion* of the left.

I recall, as a schoolboy, going to the cinema one July evening, on the day school closed down for the holidays. Deeply absorbed in the film, I suddenly noticed that I was feeling happy, and wondered why. Then I remembered: we had broken up for the holiday. The left had *forgotten*, but the right remembered.

When Maslow began talking to his students about 'peak experiences', they began talking and thinking about peak experiences. The result was that they all began having peak experiences. They began to feel that the peak experience is a normal and natural part of everyday life, and that they ought to have them more often. The left-brain arrived at this conclusion, and passed it on to the right – which responded by providing the peak experiences.

The real problem here amounts to a leakage of energy. When I have to carry out some task, I 'summon' energy, and the right-brain obligingly provides it. While I am *deeply absorbed* in the task, there is almost no waste of energy. But if I begin to lose concentration, to get bored, it is as if the connection between a hosepipe and the garden tap began to work loose, so that half the water gets lost in spray around the tap. In people suffering from anxiety neurosis, inner-tension and self-mistrust have loosened the connection until 90 per cent of the energy gets lost – which is why the slightest effort exhausts them. If I am suddenly confronted by some crisis that awakens my sense of self-preservation, I instantly tighten the connection.

Human beings have become so accustomed to a poor connection, so accustomed to inner-chaos and inefficiency, that they accept the energy-wastage as inevitable. States of primal perception, of sexual intensity, make them aware that this is untrue. The answer lies in tightening up the connection.

To grasp the full implications of this insight, we must look again at the case of the double-ambiguity planaria, mentioned in the last chapter. When the water was drained off from their tube, they were filled with alarm, and their instinct led them to rush off in search of water. For a few minutes, they were filled with panic, and would have been prepared to search for a long time. But they soon found water. The second time it happened, they were still alarmed – the water might not be there a second time – but they now knew which way to go.

Now that original success – finding the water down the lighted alleyway – was encoded by the 'robot', which noted the amount of effort required. You could think of it as a slip of paper with the words: 'Amount of energy required to deal with emergency, 14 ergs' or whatever. Which means, in effect, that in the case of a similar emergency, the instinctive part of the worm consults its computer and says: 'This problem *is not worth* an effort of more than 14 ergs. . . .'

However, the second time the problem occurs, the worm can solve it with only half that amount of effort – 7 ergs. So the robot revises its estimate downward: 'Amount of energy to solve the problem: *not more* than 7 ergs.' By the twentieth time, the estimate is down to less than an erg. This means that, confronted with the same problem, the worm's instinct tells it that an effort of more than one erg is *not worth making*. When confronted with the same problem for the fiftieth time, it doesn't *feel* like making any effort at all; it simply experiences the worm's equivalent of 'Oh no!', and refuses to move. As a consequence, it dies: of what Shaw called 'discouragement'.

The problem, we can now see, lies in that purely *mechanical* relationship between instinct and robot. The robot actually tells instinct how much effort is 'worth making' – how much *to feel*.

If the problem requires more than a certain amount of effort and persistence to solve it, the robot places it in a new category: of problems *always* worth a major effort. This is what happened with the second lot of planaria. In this case, the mechanical alliance of robot and instinct proved to be favourable to the creature's continued existence. But it is purely a matter of chance.

This is, of course, a piece of bad design on the part of the Creator – who, according to Shaw, is still engaged in experiment. I must emphasise that the flatworm is one of the simplest of living organisms; so the 'error' – or incompetence – has crept in fairly early in the evolutionary experiment.

Any cybernetician – or computer expert – could tell us what to do. A *third* element is required, to monitor the system. That element is consciousness. Shaw says in *Man and Superman*: 'Just as Life, after ages of struggle, evolved that wonderful bodily organ the eye, so that the living organism could see where it was going and what was coming to help or threaten it, and thus avoid a thousand dangers that formerly slew it, so it is today evolving a mind's eye that shall see, not the physical world, but the purpose of Life . . .' The advantage of consciousness was that, like the eye, it could *see further*. The instinct-robot alliance was too short-sighted.

Unfortunately, this new triple-alliance was not the answer either. In the lower animals, consciousness merely plays second fiddle to instinct. It endows the creature with cunning (foresight), which gives it a better chance of survival. But it is the servant of instinct. In man, it served the same purpose until the Creator had the idea of dissociating consciousness in a separate compartment of the brain. This proved to be a brilliant idea – one of His best since creating two sexes – and led to an immediate 'evolutionary leap'. Whether, as Jaynes believes, this occurred as recently as four thousand years ago is beside the point. (The level of culture displayed by Cro-Magnon man – and even Neanderthal man – leads me to keep an open mind.) What matters is that, once ego-consciousness became separated from instinct, man began to devise ways of *storing* information. And this was of immense importance. For where knowledge is concerned, instinct is an untrustworthy ally; it tells you that *it* will remember what is important. But it doesn't. The situation is analogous to someone giving you a phone number in conversation; you don't happen to have a pencil on hand, so you say: 'Don't worry, I'll remember it . . .' And you repeat it twice to make sure. But five minutes later, it has gone. . . .

Once consciousness became separated from its old ally, it lost the old feeling of invulnerability. It began building defences and taking precautions. Writing was one of those precautions. The result was the 'knowledge explosion' that created civilisation as we know it.

We could say that the pessimistic view of human existence made its appearance after the split-brain. From the point of view of intellectual consciousness, life looks oddly trivial and futile. This is because it lacks a dimension; in order to deal with the complexity of existence, the intellect reduces it to symbols, and symbols are 'flat'. Life judged by purely intellectual standards looks like vanity and misery.

Yet even here, there is another side to the coin. Aristotle may have felt that 'it is better not to have been born'; but poet-philosophers like Plato had a glimpse of a far wider horizon. They came to feel that ideas are fascinating *in themselves*, and that a man who devotes his life to ideas will eventually achieve a kind of god's-eye vision. Plato's *Symposium* is a hymn to the human mind. He is saying, in effect: 'Don't be discouraged because the way of consciousness is difficult. Press on, and you'll find that it will be more worth while than you can even imagine. . . .' Plato had glimpsed those moments of 'feedback' between left and right that make us aware that there is no fundamental contradiction: that this *is* the way of evolution.

Plato, of course, was the exception – as men of genius always are. For the rest of the human race, the new divided consciousness was a misery. For where the intelligent man is concerned, intellect is a spoilsport. The left-brain spends much of its time behaving like a nagging housewife, telling us what *not* to do. This is what D. H. Lawrence was complaining about. The cave man at least knew what he wanted; he grabbed an attractive girl and removed her tiger-skin; modern man needs half a dozen stiff drinks before he can behave as naturally. The left-brain is virtually his gaoler. But the 'natural man' is even worse-off. In a world where intelligence is more important than instinct, he simply feels a misfit – Eugene O'Neill wrote his epitaph in *The Hairy Ape*.

Moreover, the old alliance between instinct and robot is very nearly as fatal for man as it was for the flatworm. The alliance works best – as we have seen – for crisis-situations. But the whole aim of civilisation is to prevent crises arising. So modern man spends much of his time in the situation of the flatworm – bored by the repetition of the same old problems, and unable to summon the energy to deal with them, or summoning so little that he gets ulcers. Like his remote ancestors, modern man is magnificent when faced with a real challenge. War brings out the best in him; it makes him feel alive. But this has the dangerous result of leading him to seek out challenges. The left-brain has discovered that the best way to make its 'silent partner' disgorge energy is to look around for fresh stimuli. The bored child switches on television. The bored adult lights another cigarette or pours himself another drink. The bored Don Juan looks for another girl to seduce. The bored teenager joins a motor-cycle gang. And the bored Marquis de Sade, failing to see that all this dependence on stimuli is subject to the law of diminishing returns, looks around for new crimes to commit – at least, in imagination. Clearly, the idea of adding a third partner to the old instinct-robot alliance was not such an inspiration after all.

Still, we should think twice before blaming the Creator. There is nothing fundamentally wrong with the idea of a third partner. Our real problem is that the triple-alliance has *not* replaced the old instinct-robot combination. For all practical purposes, these two ancient allies still dominate human existence. Consciousness is virtually a sleeping partner. For the majority of living creatures, it is little more than a look-out, a man-in-the-crow's-nest. Instead of becoming the partner of instinct, it has accepted a position as office boy.

The proof is that the split-brain operation makes so little difference. When it was first performed, in the 1930s, the patient seemed unchanged, except that he no longer had epilepsy. And this, on reflection, is understandable. For what use *do* we make of the right-brain in everyday life? Half an hour ago, I needed my cheque book, and I had a vague memory of seeing it somewhere – a purely visual memory. Unfortunately, I had not translated this observation into left-brain terms: 'My cheque book has fallen down behind the telephone.' So the visual memory was of no use; I had to search until I found it. A split-brain patient would not have had the visual memory – or rather, it would not have been able to cross the gap; but he would probably have found the cheque book just as easily.

The fact that the split-brain operation makes so little practical difference demonstrates – as Thomas Blakeslee points out – how little creative thinking is necessary in everyday life. Einstein or Beethoven would notice the difference; I might even notice it myself, since writing involves turning intuitions into words. (After a hard day's work, *I* become virtually a split-brain patient.) But most of us would get through the day without too much difficulty. And this in itself is evidence of how far we have failed to reach our evolutionary objective. Consciousness *ought* to be 'creative'; it ought to be enriched by continual support from the right. Blakeslee quotes Mozart as saying that 'When I feel well and in a good humour . . . thoughts crowd into my mind as easily as you could wish. Whence and how do they come? I do not know. . . .'

*We* know. From the right-brain, that 'other self'. And people like Mozart ought to be the rule, not the exception. Then why are they not? Because, as James says, we have a *habit* of 'inferiority to our full self'.

The real problem is that we are trapped in a kind of vicious circle. Consciousness is *intentional*. If I look at a picture, or listen to music, without 'paying attention', I do not grasp its significance. But then, where music and painting and reading are concerned, I know perfectly well that *I* have to contribute a certain amount of concentration if I wish to get at the 'meaning'. But where ordinary perception is concerned, this is not so. When I look at a tree or a cloud – or a building for that matter – I do not feel that there is 'more to it than meets the eye', that if I wish to grasp its significance, I must make a determined effort of concentration. I assume I am simply seeing 'what is there'. Jacob Boehme would tell me I am quite mistaken. If I looked at a tree or cloud in a proper state of perception, I would be overwhelmed by its meaning. And my own experiences of sudden relief after crisis – described in the last chapter – make me aware that he is right. But my ordinary perception is limited because the amount of effort I put into it is limited. Again, we are up against that conspiracy of instinct and the robot. On the train to America, I had to *tell* myself that the scenery was beautiful, and then make a tremendous effort of concentration to make myself *see* it. *I*, the objective self, overruled the robot, and saved myself from the fate of the bored planaria. As long as we do not know this simple fact about perception – that it is a liar – we have no chance of breaking out of the vicious circle.

For of course, the key to the problem lies in that word 'meaning'. When I can *see* meaning, all the problems vanish; consciousness becomes magnificently purposeful, the right-brain performs its proper task of supporting the left, and I suddenly feel that *this* is what I was meant to do with my life. When I look at certain paintings of Van Gogh – like the Starry Night or the Road With Cypresses – I realise that he *saw* meaning as he painted them. Yet his letters make it clear that he was not able to control it, to turn it on at will; it seems to have been some kind of freak perception, due to tension and self-torment. This seems to be the trouble with meaning-perception and the peak experience – we have to wait until they knock on the door.

Or do we? On that London train, I succeeded in doing it the other way round: starting from a conviction that the meaning was *there*, and then bullying my senses until they opened-up and saw it.

The real villain, I repeat, is that alliance between instinct and the robot, which tells us that things 'are as they are', that today will be like yesterday and the day before, that human beings were *meant* to be weak and oddly limited. But although this 'unholy alliance' is the root of the trouble, it is not here that we should lay the blame. The blame should be laid squarely on the 'objective mind', the left-brain ego, for being habitually passive and feeble, and failing to play its proper part.

Consider again Greene's 'whiskey priest' in front of the firing squad. Why does he suddenly realise that it would have been 'so easy to be a saint'? Because his 'objective mind', confronted with the prospect of extinction, wakes up with a shock, and recognises that *it* is the controller of consciousness, the helmsman. Greene himself achieved the same insight when, as a bored teenager, he played Russian roulette. In 'The Revolver in the Corner Cupboard' he describes how he placed the muzzle against his right ear and pulled the trigger; when there was just a click he experienced 'an extraordinary sense of jubilation'. 'It was as if a light had been turned on . . . and I felt that life contained an infinite number of possibilities.'

But then, Greene failed to grasp the meaning of this insight: that the world blazed with meaning when the personal ego takes its proper place as the controller of consciousness. It is, admittedly, appallingly difficult to grasp, since our lives are based upon the *premise* that consciousness is the passive observer. Yet once it has been pointed out, it is easy enough to recognise that this *is* the meaning-content of our 'moments of vision'. Proust, tasting the tea-soaked cake that revived memories of childhood, says: 'I had ceased to feel mediocre, accidental, mortal.' In the sexual orgasm, we experience a blaze of certainty, of inner *power*. (It may be significant that the pineal gland, the probable source of the ecstasy, occupies a midway position in the brain.) On holiday, we begin to enjoy life because the prospect of 'newness' has galvanised us to *extra effort*. And as we exert ourselves to achieve a higher level of dynamism, we also increase the intentionality of perception; we turn the gaze into a 'seeker of meaning'.

In short, the most important factor in 'vision' is the precise *knowledge* of what you are trying to achieve. Greene achieved the knowledge – as a flash of right-brain recognition – but failed to translate it into left-brain terms. He even repeated the Russian roulette experiment several times, in an attempt to pin it down; he admits that the effect finally wore off, so that instead of a vision of infinite possibility, he felt only a 'crude kick of excitement'.

In *New Pathways in Psychology*, I have told the story of a woman friend who, tormented by the discovery of her husband's infidelity, tried to make up her mind whether to accompany him to a new job in another state, or to go with her brother to the mid-west. One day, as she was agonising over this decision, it suddenly struck her: 'I don't have to do either. *I am free.*' She says it came like a revelation, and brought an instant and tremendous feeling of relief. She said it even improved her game of tennis.

Here we can see clearly what happened. Her indecision was based upon the premise that she would be passive, and would do what either her brother or husband suggested. This 'passive fallacy' is, as we have seen, the outcome of the instinct-robot alliance, which we take absolutely for granted. But the misery of the situation and the mental strain involved finally led her to overrule the 'robot'. If her life was going to be turned upside down, then it might as well be on her own terms. Suddenly, her central-ego was in control, and she experienced Greene's insight that life was full of infinite possibilities. Greene had experienced it at the cost of considerable danger. She experienced it at the cost of some mental agony, but no danger. And there is no reason why, once the mechanism is grasped, it should involve either danger or agony. Once you *know* that 'you' should be in control of consciousness, and you make a determined effort in that direction, the rest follows inevitably.

Maslow's major mistake was in his assumption that we cannot achieve the peak experience through effort; he believed that the mechanism is too subtle to be controlled by the will. If Hudson and Miller are right, Maslow was wrong. It is true that I cannot now launch myself into a peak experience as I sit typing this page; but that would be like expecting to do a high jump from a sitting position. What I *am* asserting is that, once we understand the basic techniques, we can achieve the peak experience as predictably as a good athlete can achieve the high jump.

In a book called *The Man Without a Shadow* I stated: 'Human beings are like grandfather clocks driven by watch springs', and in a later book on Gurdjieff, added the simile of an enormous watermill driven by a muddy trickle of water. The muddy trickle is the consciousness of the 'objective mind', the left-brain ego. Yet, as we all know, the muddy trickle can be converted into a roaring torrent by a consciousness of purpose or anticipation of delight. There is nothing *inherently* wrong with the mechanism of consciousness. The trouble lies in its mistaken assumption that it is merely the man-in-the-crow's-nest, the office boy.

This same observation provides the explanation of a puzzle that has obsessed me for the past three decades: what I have labelled the 'if-only' feeling. When confronted with some crisis, or something we badly want, we feel 'If only I could solve this problem, I could maintain this sense of purpose indefinitely.' Hans Keller, the director of the BBC's music programme, has told how, in the late 1930s – when his Jewish friends were vanishing into German concentration camps – he thought: 'If only I could escape from Germany, I swear I would never be unhappy for the rest of my life.' In such moments, it seems perfectly clear that we possess the secret of happiness. Sudden relief or delight makes us aware that the ego is the boss, not the office boy. But the next morning, when we wake up and ask 'How do I feel today?', the awareness has already been abandoned in favour of the usual assumption that 'happiness' is determined by the body and the emotions.

This also explains the observation of Fichte: 'To be free is nothing; to *become* free is very heaven.' When 'I' am in control, I am conscious of freedom. When the instinct-robot alliance takes over, freedom vanishes. So when I have a 'free day' in front of me, I may view the prospect with boredom. If I wave goodbye to a car-load of departing guests, and mutter: 'Thank God, a free day at last', the freedom shimmers and glitters with potentiality. Moreover, for the next twenty-four hours I do not need to keep reminding myself that I am free; the right-brain has 'got the message'.

The sense of freedom is 'right-brain awareness'. Left-brain awareness is always active, like being 'in gear'; when a crisis vanishes, we relax, and there is a feeling of 'going out of gear'. When I start to take my freedom for granted, this no longer happens. The problem could be compared to my lawnmower, which has a powerful spring to release the gear. Recently, the spring broke, so the mower stayed in gear all the time; if I wanted to disengage it, I had to stop the engine and turn it upside down. It seems that human consciousness has a broken spring. If we could repair the spring, freedom would *always* be active and delightful. The broken-spring image also explains why most Utopian ideologies fail in practice. It is not true that all human evils will vanish once we have a just society and ample food supplies. While man lacks that 'spring', he cannot wholly dispense with the negative stimulus of problems and obstacles; they maintain his sense of meaning. It is a sad admission to have to make; but it is the key to the strange human appetite for 'complications', even for suffering.

In fact, the 'spring' of consciousness is not broken; it is just too weak. And this is a problem that can be cured. Consciousness itself is the key. When Maslow's students began to think and talk about peak experiences, they began having more peak experiences. They *assumed* that peak experiences are a natural part of life; the 'subjective mind' accepted this suggestion by the 'objective mind', and provided them with more peak experiences.

The life of the Hindu saint Ramakrishna furnishes a more extreme example. As a child, he was subject to sudden ecstasies; on one occasion he was so overwhelmed by the beauty of a flock of white cranes against a black storm cloud that he fainted. He later became a priest in the temple of the Divine Mother; but the ecstasies had become a thing of the past. One day, in despair, he snatched up a sword, and was about to plunge it into his breast when 'the buildings, the temple and all vanished, leaving no trace; instead, there was a limitless, infinite shining ocean of consciousness or spirit'. He experienced a state of samadhi (God-ecstasy) and became unconscious. But from then on, he could induce samadhi simply by repeating the name of the Divine Mother.

What had happened is clear. Ramakrishna had been waiting passively for samadhi. As he seized the sword, the 'objective mind' took control; the 'subjective mind' got the message, and provided ecstasy. The 'method' is basically the same as in the case of Maslow's students.

In fact, we all know how to make use of the same technique. A teenager who is 'sent' by the latest pop singer is making use of it; so is the opera lover who is 'carried away' by the end of *Tristan* or *Aida*. The first time we hear a piece of music, we decide that it is enjoyable, but we do not actually enjoy it. By the second or third hearing, the right-brain is responding to the suggestion that this is great music by making the muscles of the scalp tingle and sending a feeling like cold water down the spine.

But there is an apparent contradiction here. Surely it is the right-brain that appreciates the music in the first place? For a person with right-brain damage, music is meaningless. This is true, and it goes to the heart of the matter. 'Ordinary appreciation' is a right-brain activity. But it can be enormously intensified by the suggestions of the left. *This* is the essence of Hudson's discovery that the subjective mind will respond to the suggestions of the objective mind.

In short, we *already possess the means* for gaining this added control of awareness. We fail to use them only because we are unaware of their power.


Let me attempt a summary.

Life on earth has been around for about two billion years. But life invented reproduction – and death – only about half a billion years ago. This is when life learned to control its instinctive processes by means of the 'robot'.

Man is not much more than two million years old. And the 'brain explosion' that turned him into earth's most dominant inhabitant occurred only half a million years ago. So the instinct-robot alliance is about a hundred times as old as ego-consciousness.

Even then, as we have seen, consciousness continued to

play the passive role, leaving all the real decisions to instinct. Somehow, it had to be *forced* to stand on its own feet. And in recent history, not many thousands of years ago, the modern 'bicameral mind' emerged. Then man's real troubles began: loss of direction, alienation, the 'divided self', neurosis, self-mistrust. In fact, it could be argued that this partitioning of consciousness was a disaster. Human life became a misery. This is why so many of the ancient philosophers, from Ecclesiastes to Aristotle, complain that life is 'vanity of vanity'.

But all this, we have seen, came about because ego refused to play its full part in the 'triple alliance'. But then, perhaps 'refused' is too harsh a word. It has failed to play its part because, like an actor who has failed to learn his lines, it is not sure what part it is supposed to be playing. It is inclined to attribute its misery and alienation to the unkindness of fate.

In fact, it is in the position of Ramakrishna's grass-eating tiger. Ramakrishna told a story of a tiger that gave birth to a cub as it sprang on a flock of sheep. The cub grew up among the sheep, and learned to bleat and eat grass. One day another tiger attacked the flock and was astonished to discover a tiger that bleated like a sheep. It grabbed it by the scruff of the neck, dragged it to a nearby pool, and made it look at its reflection, saying 'Look, you are a tiger, not a sheep.' Then it smeared blood on the mouth of the grass-eating tiger, which – slowly, and with some hesitation – came to accept its new identity.

This problem of alienation and self-division came to preoccupy philosophers only in recent centuries: Kierkegaard was one of the first to state it clearly when he wrote (in *Repetition*): 'Who am I? What am I doing here? . . . Why was I not consulted?' In the twentieth century, Sartre labelled this sense of alienation 'nausea', while Camus called it 'absurdity'. When I first became preoccupied with the problem – in the second part of the 1940s – Kierkegaard, Kafka, Sartre and Camus were the major influences on the post-war generation of intellectuals. It was natural that I should take them as my starting point when I embarked on my own analysis of the problem in *The Outsider*. Yet in the last chapter of that book, I quote Ramakrishna's parable of the grass-eating tiger. It was already clear to me that the sense of alienation and absurdity was some kind of *misunderstanding*.

What I had grasped intuitively, and what slowly formed itself into an intellectual conviction, was that misery and alienation are not laid upon us by fate. They are due to the failure of the ego to accept its role as the controller of consciousness. All our experiences of happiness and intensity force the same conviction upon us, for they involve a sense of mastery.

It struck me that if this is correct, then certain consequences should follow: that a deliberate policy of control ought to bring an immediate change in the quality of consciousness. To use my earlier simile: if we take the trouble to tighten the link between the tap and the hosepipe, so that the 'leakage' becomes minimal, then our available inner-pressure ought to rise dramatically.

A few days of constant effort convinced me that this is precisely what happens. It also brought an insight that I have been trying to assimilate ever since. I can only express it – inadequately – by saying that we have misunderstood the purpose of left-brain consciousness. It is not intended to be an 'observer', but a *gatherer of power*. William James says: 'Most of us may . . . learn to live in perfect comfort on much higher levels of power.' In fact, we *must* learn to live on a far, far higher level of power. And *that* is what the left-brain was intended for. Its far-sightedness gives it the ability to summon power. Yet it hardly makes use of this ability. It could be compared to a man who possesses a magic machine that will create gold coins; so that he could, if he wanted, pay off the national debt and abolish poverty. But he is so lazy and stupid that he never bothers to make more than a couple of coins every day – just enough to see him through until evening. . . . Or perhaps he is not lazy: only afraid of emptying the machine. If so, the fear is unnecessary. It is magical, and cannot be emptied.